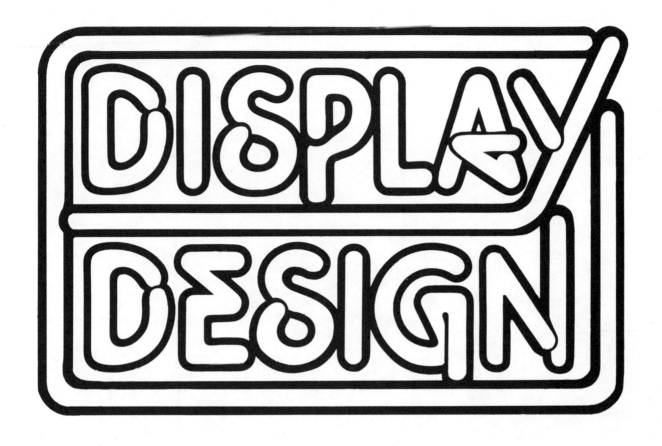

DISPLAY DESIGN

An Introduction to Window Display, Point-of-Purchase, Posters, Signs and Signage, Sales Environments, and Exhibit Displays

A SPECTRUM BOOK

Laszlo Roth

Prentice-Hall, Inc., Englewood Cliffs, N.J. 07632

Library of Congress Cataloging in Publication Data

Roth, Laszlo.
   Display design.

   (Art & design series)
   "A Spectrum Book."
   Includes index.
     1. Display of merchandise.   2. Show-windows.
I. Title.   II. Series.
HF5845.R77 1983   659.1'57   82-23184
ISBN 0-13-215491-9
ISBN 0-13-215483-8 (pbk.)

To my son, Paul Roth, and to my students at the Fashion Institute of Technology

THE ART & DESIGN SERIES. This series includes about thirty titles.

10 9 8 7 6 5 4 3 2 1

ISBN 0-13-215491-9

ISBN 0-13-215483-8 {PBK.}

Editorial/production supervision: Marlys Lehmann
Page layout: Christine Gehring-Wolf
Cover design: Hal Siegel
Manufacturing buyer: Edward J. Ellis

This book is available at a special discount when ordered in bulk quantities. Contact Prentice-Hall, Inc., General Publishing Division, Special Sales, Englewood Cliffs, N.J. 07632.

Prentice-Hall International, Inc., *London*
Prentice-Hall of Australia Pty. Limited, *Sydney*
Prentice-Hall Canada Inc., *Toronto*
Prentice-Hall of India Private Limited, *New Delhi*
Prentice-Hall of Japan, Inc., *Tokyo*
Prentice-Hall of Southeast Asia Pte. Ltd., *Singapore*
Whitehall Books Limited, *Wellington, New Zealand*
Editora Prentice-Hall do Brasil Ltda., *Rio de Janeiro*

Contents

Foreword

Within the academic environments of applied arts there are a multitude of highly technical disciplines that require an infinite amount of skills and talents toward their successful application and execution.

The disciplines of package design, visual merchandising, point-of-purchase display, graphic arts, and exhibit design all appear, at least on the surface, to be individual if not isolated areas of highly specialized design techniques. However, they are in many instances very closely related, and with an intense interrelationship that exists in the conceptual design for their successful execution.

Graphic artists, display designers, POP and package designers are often merged and married in varying degrees of talent application in singular design projects wherein the skills of many are required to bring forth a single creative commercial execution.

Professor Laszlo Roth of the Fashion Institute of Technology has prepared in his text **Display Design** a simple yet highly professional understanding of this myriad of diversified design areas and the importance of their successful integration in the difficult task of commercial/thematic designing for product presentation in an intensely competitive field. Professor Roth has successfully pierced the labyrinth of myth and misunderstanding that has historically surrounded these creative disciplines and put forth an extremely knowledgeable formula for their successful interrelationship.

Professor Roth's compassion for these arts, along with a sensitive understanding of their workings, will greatly assist and stimulate the creative skills of those who choose to follow his expert advice; this knowledge will complement them in their pursuit of design excellence.

Hugh T. Christie
Chairman, Display and Exhibit Design Department,
Fashion Institute of Technology,
New York, N.Y.

Preface

Most design-oriented persons and some young designers are not fully aware of the role of the display designer. Display design is visual merchandising.

As merchandising and retailing techniques have become more and more complex and sophisticated, so have the techniques of the wide variety of display media.

In the retail establishment, away from the mass media, the consumer and the product maker confront each other. The product maker has the product; the consumer has the money. There's an immediate result: success in making or failure to make a sale.

To design and develop window displays, posters, signage, point-of-purchase displays, selling environments, and exhibits, it takes a designer with a broad background in structural design, color studies, rendering, fashion, art history, sales, and merchandising—and above all, excellent taste.

The drama of display begins at the store windows. Decorative, elegant, sophisticated, often opulent arrangements of merchandise are presented to the consumer with the flair of a showman. More often than not, unplanned buying decisions are made in the store, and the attractive display is definitely the deciding factor in the consumer's choice.

Next to the package, the point-of-purchase (POP) is one of the most effective selling aids in retailing. In the self-service mass market, POP represents a totally visual merchandising and selling device.

Posters have always been on the borderline of fine art; they are very effective sales aids for products, the arts, exhibits, the theater, and the cinema.

Signs, especially trade signs, have a colorful history, dating back to ancient times. Signage is definitely an art form by itself. Vehicles—planes, giant trucks, vans, blimps—are moving billboards.

Environments—service stations, showrooms, fast-food restaurants, theaters, and playgrounds—are a great challenge for the designer.

Exhibits, trade shows, and fashion shows present not only products and services, but often new concepts for living and education.

The main objective of this book is to introduce the beginning designer to display design and the three-dimensional experience. There are limitless new, exciting materials—papers, foils, plastics, fabrics, and metals—as well as new technologies: projection, sound, and lighting.

Projects will be developed in the form of a scale model or a sketch. The student will experience great joy and satisfaction in total creativity and craftsmanship: designing, building, painting, photographing, and model making. Perhaps *you* will become a designer of new structural forms, unusual concepts, great fashions, dazzling costumes, and giant spectacles!

Acknowledgments

My sincere thanks to the following people who helped me in the course of preparing this book:

My colleagues of the advertising, interior design, display and exhibit design, photography, and college and community relations departments of the Fashion Institute of Technology.

Gene Moore, display director, Tiffany & Co., New York; William Mitchell, display director, Macy's, New York; Robert Ruffino, display director, Henri Bendel, New York; Ken Schlieman, director of visual merchandising, Lord & Taylor, New York; Hugh T. Christie, Fashion Institute of Technology; Howard Mont, Howard Mont Associates, Inc., Visual Communications; Etan Manasse, Etan Manasse Associates, Inc., Industrial Design; Albert H. Woods, Carlos Ramirez & Albert H. Woods, Inc.; Melvin Starr, The Artkraft Strauss Sign Corporation; Harvey Chanler, Mem Co. Inc.; Stephen Manville, photographer; G. W. Brache, Mobil Oil Corporation; Julie Salzberg, Warner-Lauren Ltd.; Emil A. Pavone, National Distillers Products Company; Bob Golby, photographer; George Wybenga, signage; J. D. Mead, Procter & Gamble; Kenneth Leonard, General Foods Corporation; Erika Gennuso, model; Steve Doyal, Hallmark Cards; Denise Ortell, Helena Rubinstein Inc.; Ethel Taub, Creative Displays, Inc.; Richard Rabkin, Ideal Toy Corporation; and William J. Vituli, The Great Atlantic and Pacific Tea Co., Inc.

CHAPTER

1

Materials, Techniques, and Tools

New materials, new techniques, and tools

Exploring and developing the creative potential

Detailed description of the variety of boards for structural design

Display papers

Display fabrics and trimmings

Mounting techniques

Adhesives

Lettering and sign making

Basic tools and materials

Art supplies

Model-making and prop-making techniques

The art of papier-mâché

Working with balsa, wood, corrugated, and Fome-Cor®

Model making with polystyrene

Thermoforming

The variety of materials available for the designer is immense. In the past, three-dimensional design was restricted to basic materials like cardboard, paper, wood, plaster, wire, glass, and fabrics. Now, however, designers have access to a wide variety of plastics: sheets, films, foams, and liquids; new fast-drying adhesives; new man-made yarns and fabrics; water-soluble permanent colors, (acrylics). Versatile, lightweight power tools save time; new reproduction methods (Xerox, color stats, transfer type) create new, exciting graphic presentations.

We live in the age of great technological development. Never before have so many diverse materials, tools, and technologies been available for the designer. Unfortunately, this

1. The computer.

1

2. Tools of the designer.

technological culture has also led to a decreasing emphasis on handwork, crafts, and individual achievement. The largest segment of our population works in industries with such minute specialization that a worker may devote his entire career to one simple operation or act, creating only a part of a product.

Personal design projects and crafts: a dress, a room, a toy for a child, all allow the individual an opportunity to feel fulfilled, having initially to conceive an idea and to carry it through every stage to completion. Experiences with materials, tools, and "hands-on" techniques allow the exploration of one's potential, so that the act of self-development and total creativity takes place.

The main objective of this chapter is to introduce the beginning designer to a variety of display materials, tools, and techniques. Some of these materials are easily available almost anywhere, others only in special shops. It is important to consult this chapter whenever you are planning a new project. Often the use of the wrong materials, tools, and techniques can create serious delays and a poor presentation. To find the source of materials and services, consult the list of suppliers at the end of the book.

Boards for Structural Design

Plywood. Plywood is an excellent material for many permanent structures. Plywood is made by laminating layers of wood veneer together. It is available in different thicknesses in most lumber yards, in 4-by-8-foot panels (standard size). Since plywood is layered, the laminated edges are visible. Tapes, veneer, or moldings can cover the edge to create a neat, finished look. Plywood should be cut with a power saw — a coping saw or jigsaw is recommended. Like most softwood, plywood should be sealed before painting with shellac or some other type of liquid sealer. Plywood takes adhesives very well (Weldwood, whiteglue, epoxy). Screws or nails are suitable for plywood.

Masonite.® This is a hardwood panel that comes in 4-by-8-foot (standard size) panels in various thicknesses. It is made of wood fibers of various densities of hardness (tempered). Masonite is available either smooth on both sides or smooth on one side and textured on the other (waffle back). It is excellent for displays and exhibits, with the ⅛-inch tempered waffle back being the best. If it is used as a large panel, Masonite should be framed on the back to prevent warpage. Framing is a simple process: strips of wood or moldings are glued along the edges of the panel, horizontally and vertically (like framing a painting). Perforated Masonite or pegboard is one of the most practical display and exhibit materials. It also comes in 4-by-8-foot panels in ⅛- and ¼-inch thicknesses. There is a wide assortment of hanging devices for racks and shelves, which are available in most lumberyards and hardware stores. Masonite is a versatile material. Like plywood, it should be cut with a power saw. It takes paint of all types, and can be attached by gluing or with nails or screws.

Homosote. Used as an insulating board for buildings. It is very practical for large panels, as it comes in 8-by-12-foot and 8-by-14-foot sizes, in thicknesses of ½ inch and ⅝ inch. The edges tend to crumble; it is advisable to frame it with molding (like a large painting). Since homosote is a rather soft material, it is excellent for bulletin boards and wall partitions. It is available in most lumberyards.

Upson Board. A trade name. Used as a wall or ceiling board. This board is a fine material for signs and cutout letters. It is ¼ inch thick and comes in 4-by-6 and 8-by-12-foot panels, in different finishes, textures, and colors. It is very easy to cut and is available in most lumberyards.

Fome-Cor.® A trade name. This is a lightweight display board with a plastic foam core. Comes in ³/₁₆-, ¼- and ½-inch thicknesses. The board has an excellent surface on which to paint or draw. The best way to cut it is with a mat knife or a blade.

Corrugated Board. Used for shipping cartons and POP displays, it comes in various thicknesses called flutings or flutes referred to as A, B, C, and E (E is the thinnest). Most POP (point-of-purchase) displays are constructed from E flute. Corrugated board comes in white or color facings, and can be painted with any type of color. It can be cut with a blade or mat knife.

Corobuff® is a flexible corrugated material, with only one side corrugated faced. It can be rolled. It is used mostly as a covering material for walls, tables, bins, and window backgrounds, and is available in many bright colors.

Cardboards. Sometimes called show cardboards, these are used for signs and posters. They come in many beautiful, bright colors in various thicknesses and sizes. The standard art-supply store size is 28-by-44 inches. There is a variety of mat boards, chipboards, and illustration boards. Board thicknesses are measured in points. The term **caliper** is used to denote thickness. It is expressed in units of thousandths of an inch (usually written decimally), which are referred to as **caliper points.** Most display constructions consists of 50-point boards. The standard illustration board is usually 60-point.

Display Papers

A wide range of solid colors, patterns, metallic papers, and specialty papers are available from your art supply store or paper merchant or distributor. Here are some of the best-known and most widely used display papers:

Seamless Papers. Seamless papers are the best product available for background or floor-covering material to cover a large area. They are widely used for window displays and by photographers for backgrounds. They come in large 8-foot and 12-foot rolls in many exciting colors.

Silk-Screened Papers. Mat papers come in many (250) colors, sold under the trade name of Color Aid.® This paper comes in 22-by-28-inch sheets. Other brands under various trade names are available in your art supply store.

Flint Papers. These are glossy, patent-leather-finish papers that come in hundreds of brilliant colors. They are occasionally used for gift wraps. They come in a standard size of 20-by-26-inches and are excellent for box wraps, pedestal coverings, and small indoor showcases (backgrounds and flooring).

There are inexpensive, but the bright colors fade if exposed to sunlight.

Foils. Foils are metallic papers, which also come laminated to boards. They are available either plain or embossed, in gold, silver, and many attractive colors and patterns.

Specialty Papers. These include tissue papers in many bright colors; parchment papers for signs; flocked, glittered, iridescent, and pearlescent papers for special effects; and mirrorlike Mylar plastic sheets for reflective backgrounds.

Display Fabrics and Trimmings

Fabrics are often used to cover backgrounds, floors, or constructions in displays, the theater, fashion shows, and exhibits.

Duvetyne. A feltlike fabric, excellent for backgrounds, it can be cut with a blade, leaving a clean edge. Duvetyne is inexpensive and is available in a wide range of colors at your display material dealer.

Burlap. Burlap is often used as a background material. It comes in assorted colors. A variation of burlap, called **monk's cloth,** comes in different textures: basket weave or small weave.

Felt. Felt is widely used in display and exhibit work, and comes in many bright colors. It

can be cut with a blade to achieve a straight edge.

Specialty Fabrics. There is a wide choice of theatrical and display fabrics: velours, satins, muslins, transparent and translucent fabrics. All are available from your display and theatrical fabric dealer.

All display and exhibit fabrics must be treated to make them fire-resistant. Request a certificate of flameproofing when you purchase your fabric, as fire inspectors require this certificate before issuing a permit for an exhibit to be set up in a public hall.

Trimmings. Ribbons, cords, laces, and trims of many different materials are often

used in various types of window displays.

Seasonal Decor. Outdoor and indoor Christmas decorations and other seasonal decor can be acquired from your local importer and manufacturer of seasonal decor. (See list of suppliers.)

Artificial Flowers and Plants. Rent or buy these from your local dealer. (Consult your telephone directory.)

Display Fixtures. Custom-built or stock display fixtures are available at your dealer, manufacturer, or distributor.

Mannequins. Custom-made or stock mannequins can be rented or bought from a mannequin maker.

Antiques. Rent or buy these from dealers and collectors.

Techniques

Background Coverings

Backgrounds, partitions, shelves, floors, and tabletops can be covered with fabrics or papers stretched over the surface and stapled on the back. A framework structure can be constructed from inexpensive lumber strippings covered with fabric. (Theatrical scenery and flats are made this way.) These lightweight, fabric-covered panels make excellent painted backgrounds for windows, stage, and fashion shows.

The entire panel can be covered with paint by spraying, using a roller or a paintbrush. Large panels are usually sprayed by commercial spraying services. The smaller panels and displays can be sprayed with a push-button aerosol can. Aerosol sprays require proper ventilation or a professional spray booth equipped with an exhaust fan. The best method to use to cover a large area with paint is the paint roller. Paint and hardware stores sell the necessary materials for roller painting. For best results, lay the panel flat on the floor or worktable.

To a lot of craftsmen the old reliable brush is still the best technique for covering displays, panels, frames, and moldings. Use flat water-based paints. Choose mat-finish paints instead of glossy ones. Shiny surfaces will reflect the light and may distract attention.

Mounting Techniques

There are several kinds of adhesives for specific jobs. In recent years the chemical industry has provided the designer with a variety of cements, glues, waxes, and adhesives. Basically there are two types of adhesives: temporary (or removable) and permanent.

One of the most popular temporary adhesives is rubber cement. It has several advantages that make it very practical and useful: It can be brushed on; the excess cement can be easily removed with an eraser (pickup type); mounted material can be removed with rubber cement thinner. Unfortunately, rubber cement is highly combustible, and must be kept away from flame or sparks.

There are several techniques for mounting with rubber cement. The best is to apply cement on the board as well as on the art, and to carefully press them together. If it is a large sheet (a poster, for example) it is advisable to use a slip sheet. Place a sheet of tracing paper or waxed paper between the board and the art, then slowly slide out the sheet while carefully pressing down the art to the board. Rubber cement has a disadvantage: Heat will cause the cement to dry out, resulting in discoloration of the paper and disintegration of the cement. Never use rubber cement to paste structural designs (boxes, pedestals, etc.) together as eventually they will come apart at the seam. There is a variation of rubber cement available in aerosol cans called Spray-Mount. This is an excellent material to use for mounting fabrics, photographs, collages, and so on.

The best permanent adhesives are the white glues. They come under various trade names (Elmer's Glue,® Sloman's Sobo).® White glue will permanently bond all porous materials — papers, boards, and fabrics — and is excellent for wood. For nonporous materials like glass, metals, or plastics, there are a variety of epoxy glues available in hardware and variety stores.

3. Mounting with rubber cement; the use of "slipsheet."

4. Staple gun.

5. Electric drill.

Professional photographers use waxed sheets to mount photos to board. There is an appliance that heats the wax on the paper and laminates it to the board permanently. Double-back adhesive tapes, pressure-sensitive tapes, push pins, and staples are all excellent devices for mounting most small signs, brochures, and photos in various ways.

Lettering and Sign Making

Although most stores have sign-making equipment, the knowledge of hand lettering is an important asset to the designer. A skilled hand letterer is always in great demand. Signs can be enlarged, reduced, or produced in large or small quantities by photostats (black and white). A small silk screen setup will produce beautiful full-color signs on interesting papers and boards. There are some three-dimensional letters made of plaster, ceramic, and vinyl that are available at your art supply store. Dry-transfer alphabets are much in demand to produce fast, elegant small signs in black and white.

Equipment, Tools, and Materials

The most practical piece of equipment for the display designer is a large working table. A 4-by-8-foot piece of ¾-inch plywood, covered with board and placed on "horses" (removable legs) can serve as an inexpensive worktable. Here are some of the basic equipment and materials you will need:

A tracing box. This is a light box with frosted glass for a top, and incandescent or fluorescent lamps mounted in the box. It is used to trace artwork and photographs or to look at transparencies and slides.

A small **silkscreen** setup, which can be used to produce quality sign cards and posters in full color.

Shelves and bins to hold art materials and equipment. These can be built easily by a handy designer.

Basic Art Supplies

Tracing papers (or pads).

Visualizing pads.

A strong **twenty-four-inch metal ruler** to use as a cutting guide.

A **T square.**

Forty-five- and ninety-degree **triangles.**

A **compass and divider.**

Some **templates:** ovals and other geometric shapes.

A **pantograph.** This is a simple device to draw enlarged or reduced duplications of artwork.

A wide assortment of **brushes,** including sign-writer brushes.

Opaque **water color paints** (tempera or showcard colors) in jars.

Acrylic paints (for glass and plastics).

Black dense **india ink** (waterproof).

Some **pencil leads** with holders (HB, 2B, 6H).

A complete set of **chisel-point markers.**

A set of color **Pentels.**

Lettering and ruling **pens** (or a Rapidograph set).

Rubber cement and **thinner.**

White glue.

Masking tape.

Papers and **boards** (optional).

Tools

In addition to the standard hand tools used by most craftsmen (hammers, screwdrivers, pliers, handsaws, drills, scissors, mat knives) one of the most important hand tools of the display designer is the stapler or the staple gun. This simple tool is used for fastening, attaching, and fabricating displays and display materials.

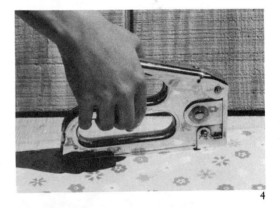

4

5

6. Sander.

7. Coping saw.

8. Working with papier-mâché: the armature.

9. Applying mâché over the armature.

10. Decorating (painting) the figure.

For power tools, the ¼-inch electric drill with attachments can be very useful. A sander and a coping saw or jigsaw are strongly recommended. Cutawl® is the trade name for a very versatile cutting machine, invaluable for the designer, which is used to cut intricate patterns from board and thin Masonite. These are basic equipment, materials, and tools to equip a busy shop for a free-lance designer or for a smaller store.

Model- and Prop-Making Techniques

Three-dimensional models and props are often built by the display artist. One of the oldest medium is papier-mâché. There are several techniques. Here is a simple one: All papier-mâché props require some sort of armature. This can be cardboard, wood, wire, or even ready-made objects (like a plastic egg or a ball). Larger props require more definite armature, usually shaped from wire mesh. The most popular method is to apply wallpaper paste to paper towels (or sometimes moist newsprint) over the armature of the prop in several layers. Rip the paper, do not cut it, to avoid sharp edges. After completion, allow it to dry at least twenty-four hours. Sand it, paint it, add additional decor or appliqué. Papier-mâché figures and props make charming displays for small showcases and windows. For variety, fabrics and decorative papers can be used for the top layer to create unusual effects. Large, lightweight 8-to-10-feet-tall figures and props can be easily built from papier-mâché.

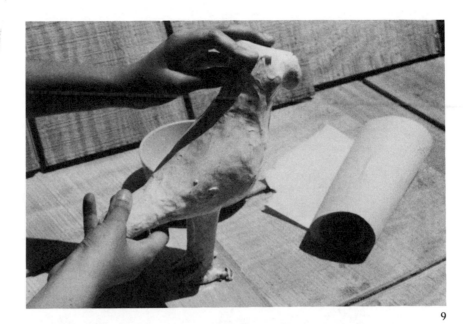

9

Model Making

Paper, cardboard, balsa wood, corrugated, and Fome-Cor® are popular model-making materials for display, exhibit designers, and architects. Intricate scale models can be built with a combination of all these materials.

10

In recent years polystyrene plastics have become more and more popular with model makers. Polystyrene is an opaque plastic sheet similar to Plexiglas. It can be cut with a blade and bonded together with a special solvent called Rez-N-Bond,® available in plastic sheet supply houses, which will bond and set instantly.

 11

11. "Leonardo" — papier-mâché figures for a slide presentation.

12. "The Three Kings" — papier-mâché figures for a slide presentation.

13. Model making with polystyrene sheets.

12

13

Polystyrene usually comes in large, 40-by-72-inch sheets; it is surprisingly inexpensive. Thickness varies from 0.20 to 250 points. For model work 0.50–0.60 point is preferable. Polystyrene can be painted or sprayed with acrylic colors or enamels. The great advantage of this material is that it will adhere instantly and is nonflammable and nontoxic. It can also be shaped with heat into curves and tubes. It is a very versatile material for the creative designer.

Thermoforming or vacuum forming is the fastest and most economical system for producing a three-dimensional object. The system is widely used in packaging for inserts, platforms, and for the popular, low-priced "blister pack."

The method is very basic and simple. A sheet of plastic is clamped in a frame, heated, and drawn into a mold by a vacuum. A temporary mold can be made of plaster, wood, or plastic. In mass production the plastic sheet can be printed, sprayed, or metallized before forming.

Small, inexpensive tabletop-type equipment is being marketed for craftsmen and designers to use for models and small runs. This is a valuable tool for the display as well as for the POP designer.

CHAPTER

2

Window Display

Historical Background

14

14. Window display, turn of the century.

Window display is as old as selling merchandise to consumers. In ancient Rome, merchants displayed their wares over their storefronts. The wares were hanging or tied with ropes to prevent thievery. This method of displaying merchandise was customary for several centuries.

In America, some of the early merchants, the traveling peddlers, decorated their wagons with their wares. The first stores of the western settlers had glass windows to display merchandise. Some of the finest storefront designs, complete with glass windows and fine, hand-lettered signs, were built in pioneer days in the West.

In the early 1900s, with the creation of the plate glass window, contemporary window display was born. Now the prospective customer on the street could see and admire the new merchandise, which was cleverly, often profusely displayed in the windows. Store windows had a cluttered, overstuffed look, as merchants displayed large quantities of goods in the windows to show variety. As merchandising and selling techniques have become more and more sophisticated, so have the techniques of window display.

21

15

The Contemporary Window Display

Retail (window) display follows demographic and technological changes. It was the widespread use of the automobile that established the shopping center with its multiple stores and services. The concept of the department store has changed considerably. Usually located in cities, these stores have a unique personality and character. They represent tradition, class, and often snobbery. The architecture is usually vertical, with several floors connected by escalators and elevators. They place great emphasis on display windows.

The shopping center is designed laterally, with almost unlimited parking space and fewer display windows. This new concept of retailing is a definite challenge to the older downtown store. It is the permissive character of the suburban shopping center that has attracted the young, informally dressed shoppers, while in the older, more traditional department store shoppers have tended to dress accordingly.

Then came the discount house, with its magic appeal: low price. Here display is an

15. Storefront and windows, 1896 advertising.

16. Shopping center.

17. Self-service store. Courtesy of The Great Atlantic & Pacific Tea Company, Inc.

22

important selling aid. With the use of the computer, self-service became the main feature of the discount store. Inventory systems, modern fixture design, and sensible prices all helped the consumer choose the right merchandise for the right price. Whether it is an elegant department store, a lively shopping mall, a busy discount store, or a chic boutique, display has become indispensable because it attracts attention. Display presents merchandise dramatically and the merchandise sells. It is no longer a matter of **how much** merchandise is shown, but **how** it is shown. Display is big business. The display designer must be able to design, build, and install displays; he or she must be the creative member of the store's promotional planning team. The education of the display designer should consist of sound training in the art of drawing, rendering with markers, lettering, structural design, and art history (the history of styles). The designer should visit the theater, the cinema, art galleries, museums, and must be an observer of the current scene — art, music, and fashion. These studies develop taste, creativity, and sophistication, the primary requisites for a display designer.

16

17

18. Window styles: island front, angled front, straight front window. Drawings by Paula Drohosky.

19. Shadowbox showcase by Kathi Schauer, Fashion Institute of Technology (F.I.T.) student.

20. Shadowbox showcase, close-up, by Kathi Schauer, F.I.T. student

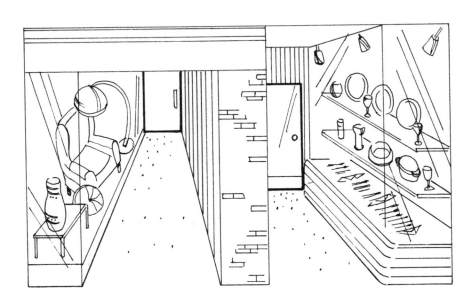

The Store

There are several styles and variations in the store and storefront design. Windows basically fall into one of the three general types: straight, angled, or island.

The **straight** front-window structure runs parallel to the sidewalk. **Angled** fronts usually follow the sidewalk contour (corner or L-shaped windows). **Island** fronts are windows that can be viewed from all sides, usually constructed to form an arcade. The arcade allows the shopper to walk around the windows. Arcade fronts are most relaxing for the shopper, and can be decorated with great imagination and creativity.

Modern suburban stores and shopping centers utilize open-back windows, through which the shopper can see the interior of the store. Here, window displays are specially designed to blend with the interior design of the store.

Some store windows have built-in elevators (Lord & Taylor in N.Y.C.) that enable the designer to create exciting visual effects. These windows are usually located above the display department. The platforms can be lower, decorated, and then raised to the desired elevation.

Elevated windows are built about one to two feet above the sidewalk.

Lobby windows help to lead customers into the store or to present merchandise in busy lobbies of buildings.

Shadowbox windows are usually shallow, vertical cases, often used in hotel lobbies to display luxury items.

Horizontal cases are widely used in shops as well as in museums and exhibits.

Interior Display Areas

21. Table arrangement. Courtesy of Warner/Lauren Ltd. Cosmetics.

22. Gourmet boutique, Henri Bendel, New York. Robert Ruffino, display director.

23. Showcase by Ralph Grasa, F.I.T. student.

The furnishings and the displays of the store should be designed and placed to create the best visual impression for the customer. They should be arranged to sell merchandise and at the same time to look pleasing. Store furnishings and displays are seasonal (Easter, fall, Christmas, etc.). The furnishing of each department must be arranged by the display person to create the mood of the

particular season. Here are some of the basic display arrangements:

Corner Shops or a shop within the shop. Boutiques, kitchen shops, college shops, and beauty shops, for example, lend color to the department, create traffic, and often become an important center of selling. In recent years audiovisual effects are being utilized to create a mood (discos, for instance).

Counter and **table displays** require constant attention, since

21

there is always heavy customer traffic and displays must be rearranged periodically.

Ledges, the tops of the shelves, sometimes serve as areas for display.

Islands are open spaces usually surrounded by the sea of customers.

Discount stores and supermarkets utilize the **dump display,** where the merchandise is thrown into a container.

Department stores usually create a **display prop** or a **booth** to promote a service or to sell a product. **Islands** can be utilized with a wide variety of display mannequins and decorative panels to promote and sell goods in an atmosphere of good decor and style. **Showcases, shadowboxes,** and **display cases** of a wide variety can be placed in strategic areas. Display fixtures, stands, easels, racks, forms, millinery heads, and mannequins are all standard props of the displayman.

Mannequins first appeared at the turn of the century, when they were constructed of wax. Wax scratches easily and is damaged by temperature changes, so it was eventually replaced by papier-mâché. The modern mannequin is made of plastic; it is a veritable work of art. The mannequin is the most effective display prop, as it presents fashions on a lifelike human figure. Mannequins are made in standing, sitting, and

24. Antique mannequins from the F.I.T. galleries.

25. Mannequins by D.G. Williams, Inc.

26, 27. Contemporary child mannequins from the F.I.T. galleries.

24

reclining positions, as well as various other poses. The standard mannequin is a standing one with moveable arms, wrists, elbows, waist, and legs. Women and children mannequins are equipped with a rod and a metal or glass base to make them stand. Male mannequins usually do not have a stand. They are fitted with an adjustable bolt in the heels that maintains their balance. They wear wigs although occasionally the hair is painted or modeled in a stylized manner. They wear garments in all the popular sizes.

To dress a mannequin, certain parts can be removed (arms, waists) and replaced to assure natural fit. They should always be taken apart for moving from one area to another.

There are a variety of other display forms to present garments and accessories. Usually these are made of papier-mâché, rubber, plastic, or other materials.

25

26

27

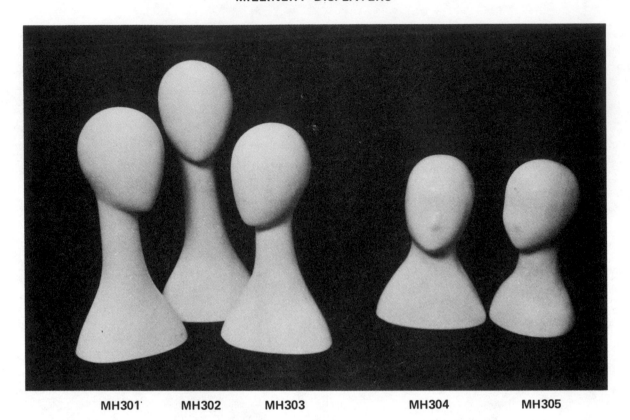

MH301   **MH302**   **MH303**   **MH304**   **MH305**

GLOVE & MILLINERY DISPLAYERS

28. Millinery and glove displayers
by Jerry Roe Enterprises, Inc.

LADIES "LEANER" FORMS

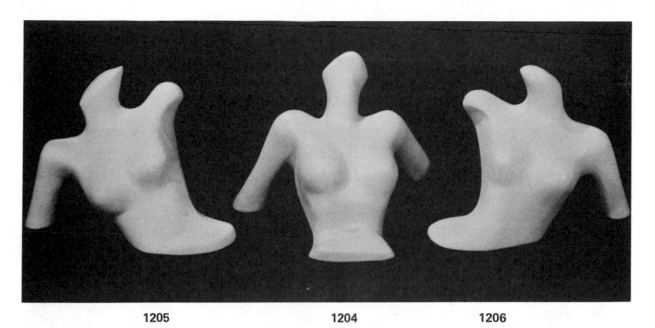

| 1205 | 1204 | 1206 |

LADIES ASSORTED FORMS

| 1601 | 1510 | 1503 | 1512 |

29. Display forms by Jerry Roe
Enterprises, Inc.

30

Proper lighting adds dramatic effect to a store window as well as to the store interior. Lighting makes merchandise more attractive, and creates mood and atmosphere for the customer. Lighting can be incandescent or fluorescent, direct or indirect. Color filters, spotlights, and floodlights can be used to create dramatic effects. Spotlights concentrate light on a given spot, while floodlights flare out or spread (flood) the area. Incandescent lighting — the bulb-and-filament type of illumination — produces heat. In a small area it might become a fire hazard. You need ample ventilation when incandescent floods or spots are used. Fluorescent lighting is cool, creating very little heat.

To achieve dramatic effects for the display window or display area, overhead or side lighting is most effective. Lighting from below may give a dramatic effect, but deep shadows may not always be suitable to create the proper mood. The use of color lighting is another method of creating an atmosphere or a mood. With the use of color filters (red, blue, amber, green) the designer can create a night setting (blue filter), dramatic or warm background (amber), mystery and contrast (green), or an emotional setting (red). Another type of filter is the gelatin, in many exciting colors; it may be used with special fixtures.

30. Lighting and display by Susan V. Guerrina, F.I.T. student.

31. Lighting and display by Denise Levine/Eleanor Scianca Lepore, F.I.T. students.

The Design Process of the Window Display

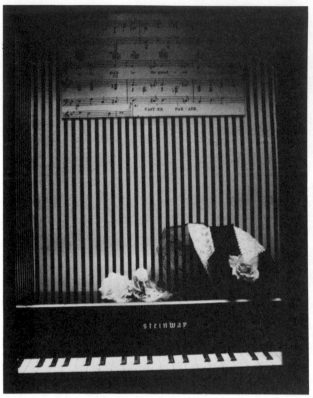

32

33

Where do ideas come from? An idea can come from anywhere, from anyone. However, a specific idea for a specific purpose can only come from a trained, disciplined mind. Searching for creative ideas to present merchandise dramatically, the designers' sources should include extensive study of the current trends, fashions, and buying habits of the public. The designer must be a regular reader of the daily newspapers, trade publications, and magazines (**Vogue, Harper's Bazaar, Mademoiselle,** and **Glamour,** among others). **Woman's Wear Daily** reports the recent fashion trends

here and abroad. Others keep the designer posted about textiles, housewares, home furnishings, and trends in accessories. Trade shows and fashion shows, galleries and exhibits are all sources of inspiration and veritable gold mines for display ideas.

The successful, attention-getting window display is a dramatic and above all a simple presentation of merchandise or services. It sells **one idea** at a time. This principle applies to fashions, accessories, and luxury items (jewelry, cosmetics, gifts). When it comes to multiple choices — footwear, hats, stationery,

housewares, home furnishings, china, glassware, and confectionary — these items could be displayed in groups and varieties without that overstuffed, cluttered look. The customer must make the choice right at the windows, not in the store (good example: shoes).

Seasonal-display arrangements and windows always sell goods. Christmas is probably the busiest and the most creative season for the designer. Windows, the interior, and the cases are transformed into a holiday atmosphere. Other important seasons for display arrangements are Easter,

34

34

35

Mother's (and Father's) Day, back-to-school, fall, Thanksgiving. Virtually every window decor has a seasonal or fashion-motivated theme. Even current news events can generate ideas.

Start with a simple thumbnail sketch, the core of the idea. Develop these sketches into full-color marker sketches. Lighting effects and the arrangement of the merchandise are clearly defined. Props and mannequins are carefully placed to enhance the appearance of the merchandise. On a large project, a scale model is built. The scale model is an expensive but excellent method of presentation of an idea or concept.

The finest and most imaginative windows are the world-famous Tiffany windows on New York's Fifth Avenue. They are basically rather small windows, presenting jewelry and precious stones. For many years now, Tiffany's internationally famous display director, Gene Moore, has commissioned designers to create unusual props and effects. The cardinal rules here are: simplicity, originality and superb taste. Here some of the finest examples.

32. Window display scale model by Randi Caropola, F.I.T. student.

33, 34, 35. Tiffany & Co., New York City, windows. Gene Moore, display director.

Windows with unusual presentations can attract millions of people. Lord & Taylor's New York store presents an annual Christmas show of animated window display, done in exquisite style. The windows of the world's largest department store, New York's Macy's, are a constant source of inspiration for a designer. Henri Bendel's New York store windows and interiors show the world's most innovative concepts of display design. Boutiques and specialty stores offer an incredible variety of creative ideas. Throughout the United States, from the large cities to the small towns, display is a serious art form wherever merchandise is offered in retail stores. Display is no longer created and installed by store clerks. Installation or trimming is done by the professional display person, the expert and specialist in this exciting, fast-moving field.

36. "The Grand Ballroom of the Ritz Carlton" hotel window display, Lord & Taylor, New York City. Ken Schlieman, director of visual merchandising.

37. "Radio City Music Hall" window display, Lord & Taylor, New York City. Ken Schlieman, director of visual merchandising.

38. Christmas interior decor, Henri Bendel, New York City. Robert Ruffino, display director.

38

39

40

41

38

42

43

39. Interior store decor, Henri Bendel, New York City. Robert Ruffino, display director.

40. Window display, Henri Bendel, New York City. Robert Ruffino, display director.

41. Store interior, Henri Bendel, New York City. Robert Ruffino, display director.

42. The Silo Boutique, New Milford, Conn. Photo by Katrina Johnson.

43. The Silo Boutique — merchandise arrangement. Photo by Katrina Johnson.

Behind the Scenes: The Display Department

Most department and specialty stores have their own display department, headed by the display director or the display manager. The shop has large worktables, equipped with power and hand tools. Some of the larger stores have their own carpentry shops to build sets and props. There is a storage area for props, display forms, and mannequins; a mannequin bin, with a separate compartment for each mannequin according to age and sex; a special space to dress mannequins; and a space to paint or spray props. There is also the sign shop for sign making; and there must be a storage area for display materials: fabrics, seamless papers, boards, plastics, artificial flowers, and decorative materials. In addition, there is a storage place for tools and paint. Today's display person is a professional, and in order to be effective, he often finds himself a jack-of-all-trades.

The Technique of Window Display: Installation and Trimming

Neatness is the most important consideration in designing and installing displays. The word **trim** is almost synonymous with **neat**. Here are some of the basic rules:

1. Always wear window socks or remove shoes before entering display areas.
2. Check and double-check displays for lint, dust, flakes, pins, thread, and so on.
3. Dust and inspect all props.
4. Keep window glass clean inside and outside.

Here are some of the basic categories of displays:

Woman's apparel displays

Men's apparel displays

Children's apparel displays

Home furnishing and appliance displays

Linen, china, and glassware displays

Special events and seasonal displays

Multiple or mass displays

Good composition is the most important principle of installing the retail display. **Balance** is the main element. There are two main types of balance: **Bisymmetrical** or formal, and **asymmetrical** or informal. Asymmetrical balance in display is more interesting than formal balance, as it creates more imaginative, often shocking effects, while symmetrical balance creates beautiful, formal, almost theatrical effects. Certainly there is room for both systems.

44. Food and confectionary
display, Macy's, New York City.
William Mitchell, display director.

45. Women's apparel display
(depth), Macy's, New York City.
William Mitchell, display director.

46. Women's apparel display
(angles), Macy's, New York City.
William Mitchell, display director.

47. Laura Ashley windows,
Macy's, New York City. William
Mitchell, display director.

44

45

46

47

Depth is another aspect of composition. Display is a three-dimensional art. Depth adds interest to any arrangement. Creating an illusion with artwork or by arranging merchandise at different levels and distances is a sure way of creating depth.

Repetition is often monotonous; however, mass displays (multiples) are based on the visual principle of **choice**. Shoes, hats, shirts, toys and games, or housewares can be displayed cleverly by using fixtures and props that create depth and break up the monotony of repetition.

Heights and **angles** can be devised by hanging merchandise from ceiling grids. This method can create an interesting visual effect; with the proper lighting, it can be an effective display device.

Motion is created with turntables, fans, motors, and animated figures. These devices should be used with restraint. Motion must not be based on the novelty of the idea, but on its potential for attracting the eye to the merchandise and for creating sales.

Window Signs A display without good copy is like a news photo without the caption. Signs are silent salesmen. They can do a good job of selling because they can provide follow-through to ads and TV promotions. Signs may be large or small, made of cutout letters or printed, but they must be eye-catching, with clever, interesting copy.

48. Swim wear windows, Macy's, New York City. William Mitchell, display director.

49. American sportswear designers window display, Lord & Taylor, New York City. Ken Schlieman, director of visual merchandising.

50, 51. Children's apparel display at the F.I.T. galleries.

48

49

50

51

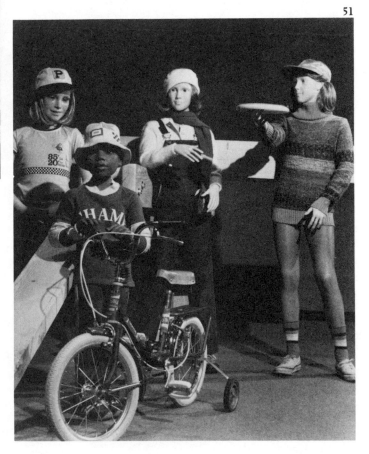

New Options for the Designer

Department stores, specialty stores, shops, even large supermarkets all use the services of the display man or woman. Most employers pay premium rates to display personnel with outstanding abilities and talent. An increasing number of schools are introducing display courses, which train the student in various display techniques. The course often includes designing and staging fashion shows and floats for parades, and television presentations.

For the young designer there are great opportunities waiting in this lucrative field: staff jobs with a store or free-lance display work with the small shops. Free-lance design can be a highly profitable and rewarding field; however, it requires a more businesslike attitude in order to succeed. It is advisable to obtain a written contract from free-lance accounts. This should consist of a document (or letter) stating the terms of the job: hourly rates or flat rates, a retainer for a specific period of time (six months, a year, etc.), cost of props, materials, transportation, and so on. Misunderstanding of terms can cost time and money.

In most large cities there are importers and manufacturers of display materials. With this service and the designer's own specially designed and built props and decorations, a talented and ambitious person can start a profitable display career. Business ability and salesmanship are assets.

Project Number 1

Christmas is the busiest season for the display designer. The design, creation, and construction of windows and props takes months of hard work and planning. Like all design projects, window displays start with preliminary design concepts in sketch form. The sketches present the concept and the theme of the window. The Christmas windows of a department store must have a theme, and it often takes several windows to carry out the story. Fairy tales, Christmas stories or poems, the ballet, the opera, Victorian or contemporary settings can all be utilized here. In the Christmas windows the merchandise becomes secondary. The windows serve as a public service; they create a festive Christmas mood and spirit for the prospective customer.

It would be exciting to build a scale model with a proscenium (theater stage front) from a cutout board or Fome-Core. Create a lavishly decorated set, complete with figures (cutouts). Use a shadowbox that represents the depth of the window. Leave the top of your "stage" open for your light source (battery-powered flashlight bulbs). Your scale should be one inch to one foot. Create an entire storefront — at least four windows — to tell your Christmas story.

Project Number 2

This is a serious and practical project. Create the following window display concepts in a full-color sketch form:

1. A back-to-school concept that presents fashions and accessories for young people of high school and college age. Use mannequins and props to display clothing and accessories. Create a simple, yet strong visual impact. The actual sketch should be 14-by-17 inches, matted in a contrasting color for presentation. Use your best medium — markers, designers' colors, or watercolors.

2. A small showcase to present a nationally advertised fragrance. Here, total simplicity and sophistication are required. Use minimal props. Your color, lighting, and background should enhance this precious merchandise.

3. Create a Tiffany's type of small jewelry window. The theme is important here. Study the enclosed photos and create an original, stunning window!

Books to read (and look at):

Buckly, Jim. **The Drama of Display.** N.Y., N.Y.: Pellegrini & Cudahy, 1953.

Joel, Shirley. **Fairchild Book of Window Display.** N.Y., N.Y.: Fairchild Publications, 1973.

Pegler, Martin M. **Language of Store Planning & Display.** N.Y., N.Y.: Fairchild Publications, 1982.

Pegler, Martin M. **Store Windows that Sell I–II.** N.Y., N.Y.: Retail Reporting, 1982.

Rowe, Frank A. **Display Fundamentals.** Cincinnati, Ohio: Signs of the Times Publishing Co., 1970.

Windows at Tiffany's, The Art of Gene Moore. N.Y., N.Y.: Harry N. Abrams, Publisher, 1980.

CHAPTER

3

The Point-of-Purchase Display

The development of the POP display

Early POP fixtures

Consumer buying habits in the past and today

New selling techniques

Mass marketing and the self-service system

All categories and types of POP displays and fixtures

The production technique of the POP display

Basic corrugated board technology

Plastics, wood, and metal

Molding and fabricating

Printing and assembly

By the middle of the nineteenth century brand names began to appear, and manufacturers of consumer products started to develop signs, fixtures, and containers bearing the name of their products. It was considered quite prestigious to display these in the store.

At first these "fixtures" were mostly large containers, barrels, boxes, and storage cabinets. They held basic commodities: tea, crackers, flour, notions, and patent medicines.

In the United States, tobacco companies developed a truly American symbol for a point-of-purchase display: the cigar store Indian, the first effective outdoor point-of-purchase display. Six feet tall, hand carved from white pine, wearing buckskin leggings and moccasins, this Indian usually wore a feathered headdress and held a bunch of cigars in one hand. The figure was elaborately painted and decorated, occasionally gilded. It is estimated that between 1850 and 1890 about twenty-thousand Indians were carved. Today, the wooden Indian is a valuable collector's item.

Metal and wood cabinets to hold various consumer goods

52

53

54

52. Early packages with brand names. Courtesy of Landor Associates.

53. An early (1906) package — POP. Courtesy of Landor Associates.

54. The American cigar store Indian. From the author's collection.

were much in demand by the stores. Clocks were decorated with brand names; large glass jars that held hard candies and peanuts became standard fixtures for the store.

With the rapid growth of our industries and the variety of products, selling techniques have radically changed. The point-of-purchase display became an effective selling aid for the retailers. By 1910, die-cut three-dimensional displays began to appear. Photographic displays made their appearance in the late 1920s. With the development of the new plastic materials and techniques, point-of-purchase displays can now be produced in a variety of styles for practically all consumer goods.

Our contemporary POP display is a long step from the early cigar store Indian. Its importance has increased with the growth of retailing and the needs of mass marketing. The expansion of the self-service stores and the change in consumer buying habits both contributed to the development of POP materials. Often, unplanned buying decisions are made in the store, and effective, well-designed displays of merchandise are deciding factors in consumers' choice.

55. An early (1896) display case. From the author's collection.

56. A 1910 die-cut display card. From the author's collection.

57. A 1907 calendar (premium).

58. The self-service store with POP displays. Courtesy of The Great Atlantic & Pacific Tea Company, Inc.

55

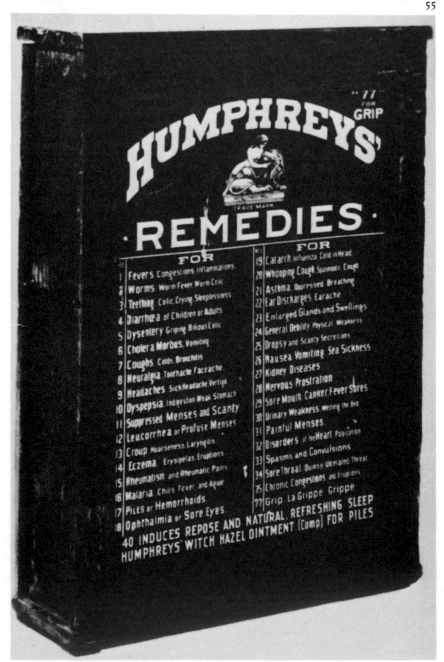

58

There are several categories of POP displays, each serving a specific merchandising function. Each category has its own variations, depending on its purpose and location.

The modern retail establishment is a busy place. A large percentage of selling is self-service, whereby consumers pick and choose the merchandise themselves rather than having it brought to them by salespeople.

Display merchandisers play an important part in the self-service system because these are strategically placed in the store, usually near the cash register or the checkout counter. The display merchandiser is sometimes called a **promotional display,** because it is designed for use only for a duration of a particular promotion. Promotional displays have a short life, usually three to four weeks. The materials used are usually corrugated board (E flute) combined with inexpensive vacuum-formed platforms to hold products.

The **display shipper** is the most basic variation of the promotional display. It is a shipping carton that opens up to form a display with a die-cut riser (or reader) panel for art and copy. Shippers are used for mass-merchandising health and beauty aids, liquor, toys, and books. The advantage of the shipper is that it is a combination of a shipping carton and a display setup.

Another popular variation is the **dump bin,** which is designed to stand on the floor, filled with merchandise. Typical examples of dump bins can be seen in supermarkets and liquor stores. Another type of dump bin is made of a more permanent material, wire. Wire units can hold heavy and bulky merchandise (bottles, jars), and they are reusable.

60

62

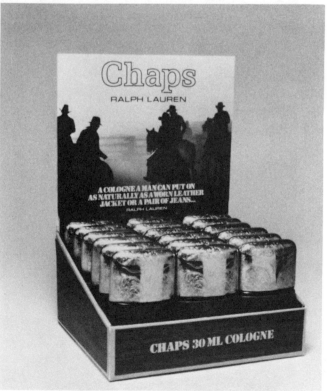

61

59. Display shippers. Courtesy of Helena Rubinstein, Inc.

60. Promotional counter display and shipper. Courtesy of Mem Company, Inc.

61. Counter display shipper. Courtesy of Warner/Lauren Ltd. Cosmetics.

62. Counter display. Courtesy of Warner/Lauren Ltd. Cosmetics.

63. Pole display. Courtesy of E.J. Brach & Sons/Creative Displays.

64, 65. Floor stands. Courtesy of Hallmark Cards, Inc.

66. Rotating floor stand. Courtesy of Cool Ray/Personal Care Brands, Division of Warner/Lambert Company.

67. Corrugated floor stand. Courtesy of Prentice-Hall, Inc.

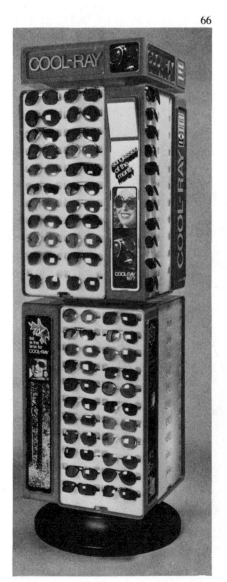

66

Pole display is mounted on a footed pole, usually a long paper tube. Often it is used in combination with another type of display, usually to elevate the "reader." **Pole toppers** arc clever die-cut graphics, especially popular in supermarkets and liquor stores.

Promotional-display categories offer a number of clever combination displays. The **motion** or **animated display** works with a small battery-operated electric motor. Motion is an exciting aspect of display, one that really stops the consumer. Hanging displays like **mobiles** are most effective. They can be made of board, inflated vinyl, or vacuum-formed lightweight plastics.

Floor stands are large displays that the dealer has to set up. One of the ways to insure getting floor space for your product and display is to send the merchandise to the dealer with some kind of special promotional offer to the consumer or a special incentive to the dealer. This type of display is called a **premium display**. Send-away premiums can be actual merchandise, housewares, appliances, toys, gifts, or books. The display unit usually displays the samples and a form to send away for the offer. These promotions are backed up with heavy print and television advertising. See also Figures 68–73 on the following pages.

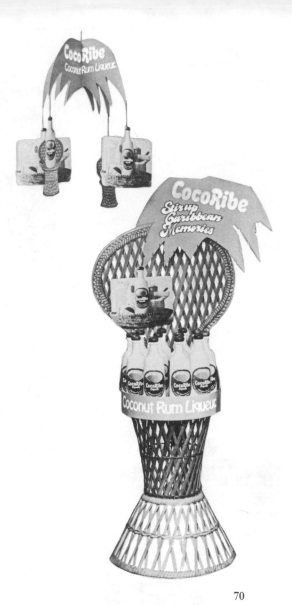

68   69   70

68. Old Grand Dad Father's Day case card display shipper. Courtesy of National Distillers Products Company.

69. Dealer loader/dealer incentive Old Taylor stove display. Courtesy of National Distillers Products Company.

70. Dealer loader/dealer incentive Coco Ribe wicker bin display and mobile. Courtesy of National Distillers Products Company.

71. Dealer loader/dealer incentive Grande Marque wine rack display. Courtesy of National Distillers Products Company.

72. Jell-O premium display. Courtesy of General Foods Corporation.

73. Zest premium display. Courtesy of Procter & Gamble.

71

72

73

The **dealer incentive** or **dealer loader** is used to help sell a promotion to the store. The display is designed around some useful unit for the dealer, such as a cart, bridge table, bench, deck chair, or other useful article or object.

Counter display is the popular name of most promotional displays, because they are placed on the counter. These are self-service units of various sizes. Drugstores display a variety of types of counter displays.

Permanent displays serve the same function as the promotional display. They are designed to insure a permanent space in the store. These can be restocked with merchandise. Permanent units range from a simple wire rack used for books and greeting cards to well-designed expensive fixtures.

Shelf extenders and **shelf dividers** are permanent trays to arrange and organize the product and package. They are fastened or clamped to the shelf, or occasionally project from it.

Gravity-fed displays are one of the oldest display systems. They are used for small packages, confectionary, films, hardware, and so on. These units can be hung on walls or can stand on counters.

Some of the finest examples of permanent displays are cosmetic displays. They are exquisitely designed, often in the shape of a display cabinet to hold merchandise, usually makeup products or fragrances. In addition to displaying the product, they contain color charts showing the range of colors in the line. Department stores rarely use this type of display, but they are supplied with a **tester,** a small display unit with a fragrance bottle, a sort of "help yourself" for the customers. Makeup testers are

59

74

75

76

74. Permanent display (gravity-fed). Courtesy of Helena Rubinstein, Inc.

75. Gravity-fed display. Courtesy of Warner/Lauren Ltd. Cosmetics.

76. Shelf-extenders, dividers, and signs. Courtesy of The Great Atlantic & Pacific Tea Company, Inc.

77. Dump-bin wire display. Courtesy of Brand's Fine Flavours.

78. Tester. Courtesy of Warner/Lauren Ltd. Cosmetics.

79. Lipstick tester. Courtesy of Helena Rubinstein, Inc.

77   78

79

also very popular small displays on department store counters. With a trained cosmetician in attendance, the customer is encouraged to test and try the product. This type of display is usually made of Lucite with gold hot stamping, and is an expensive, but very elegant, unit.

Wire displays are permanent or semipermanent displays. These are rotating or stationary floor stands. There are several rack systems available. They are usually six feet high, made of welded wire and plastic, and equipped with hooks or shelves. They can be supplied with a "reader" on the top. Wire displays are used for a wide assortment of types of merchandise: hardware, toys, books, stationery, notions, housewares, cosmetics, and confectionary. Although they can be custom built, there are hundreds of different models of inexpensive stock wire displays manufactured.

Rotating displays, made of permanent plastics and used for watches, sunglasses, and accessories, are often used in exhibits and retail stores. They carry an entire line of merchandise. Floor stands take very little space and enable the customer to browse and select the proper merchandise.

There are large semipermanent displays for showrooms and service stations, used to present large appliances, automobile accessories, tools, and machinery. These are fixtures that can be used either indoors or outdoors.

Producing the Point-of-Purchase Display

A competent designer cannot function without a basic knowledge of materials and manufacturing processes. Planning and designing a POP display is a complex job involving a variety of materials and technologies. Paper, board, corrugated board, plastics, and various printing methods all play an important part in the production of the display.

The most practical and widely used material for temporary displays (merchandisers, promotional displays) is corrugated board. This was originally part of an article of clothing: The famous gentlemen's top hat of the nineteenth century was fashioned with a band of "fluted paper." In 1874 Oliver Long, an American inventor, sandwiched the fluted paper between two paperboard sheets. This was the beginning of a new industry: corrugated board. Today the corrugated industry employs about 118,000 people in 1,427 plants; it is a $10 billion industry. It is the largest industry of the paperboard (often called fiberboard) field. The largest market is for shipping containers used by every industry in the United States. Corrugated is lightweight and strong,

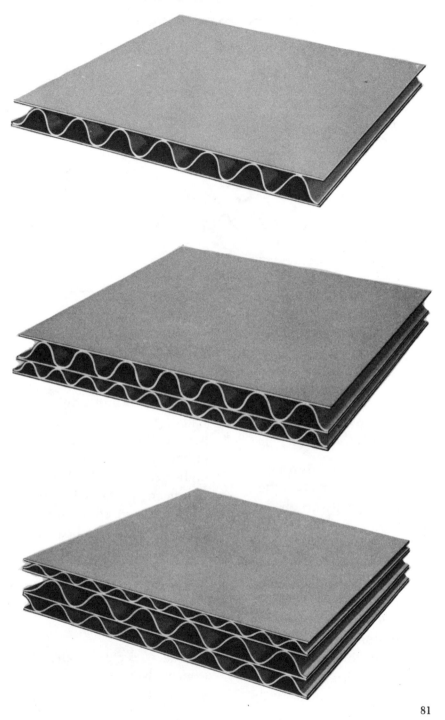

81

81. Corrugated board. Courtesy of the Fibre Box Association.

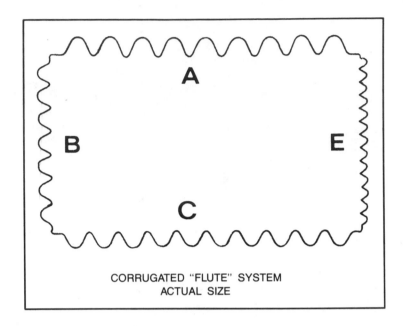

CORRUGATED "FLUTE" SYSTEM
ACTUAL SIZE

82. Corrugated board "flute" gauge. Courtesy of the Fibre Box Association.

therefore it is most suitable for the construction of the POP display.

Four flute structures are available. A flute has the greatest capacity to absorb shock, due to wider spacing of flutes. B flute has the greatest number of flutes per foot to provide maximum crush-resistance. C flute combines the properties of A and B flutes. E flute is a very thin corrugated board, used in packaging and for most large or small sturdy displays. E flute can be impregnated and coated with various waxes and plastics. It can be successfully printed and screened. The most important advance in

corrugated printing in recent years has been the use of flexographic printing, which utilizes quick-drying inks and high-speed presses. Another significant trend is toward greater use of colors on clay-coated white liner boards. The use of preprinted liners and full-color lithographed labels laminated to the board can create an attractive full-color display.

Unlike package design (especially in folding-carton construction), POP displays have a very limited number of standard patterns. Most displays are unique, cleverly conceived and constructed. Assembled by the storekeeper, they must be

simple structural designs. It takes a designer with a thorough knowledge of structural design to develop a functional POP display.

The chemical industry has provided the designer with a new material — plastics. We live in the age of plastics. Plastics are chemically synthesized from crude oil, coal, natural gas, air, water, trees, soybeans, and cotton. They are divided into two groups: **thermoplastics,** which can be softened or recycled by heat, and **thermosets,** which, once molded, cannot be softened for further processing or recycling. Plastics can be liquid, flexible, transparent, and opaque. They can be made in any specified color; they come in films and fibres. Plastics can be molded, extruded, shaped and fabricated from sheets.

Molding is one of the simple ways of shaping plastics into objects or forms. There are several methods of molding, depending on the item to be made and the type of plastic used. Most permanent displays are made by **injection molding.** It is used only for themoplastics. The plastic resin (granules or powder) is first melted in a heating chamber and then forced by a plunger into an injection molding machine. When the plastic has set in the mold, the mold opens and the product is ejected.

The mold then closes again and the process is repeated. In injection molding, too, often plastics are used to imitate other materials. They can simulate metal, glass, or wood. Because of their chemical composition, plastics are not restricted to the same forms that the real material has to take. Working with plastics can be a truly creative experience. The cost of injection-molded displays is relatively high compared to another popular system, **thermoforming or vacuum forming,** which shapes with heat and vacuum. The shaping of the heated themoplastic sheet or film occurs through forced contact with the mold.

Like most shaping processes, thermoforming is relatively simple. There are several variations of thermoforming systems available, depending on need and the type of plastics used. Most POP displays — especially the temporary, promotional type of display — use thermoformed platforms and trays to hold merchandise. The structural strength of the tray depends on the thickness of the plastic sheet.

HEATING   **FORMING**
a. Vacuum forming into a female mold
b. Vacuum forming over a male mold
c. Drape forming into a female mold
d. Drape forming over a male mold
e. Vacuum forming into a female mold with helper (plug-assist vacuum forming)

Various techniques of thermoforming

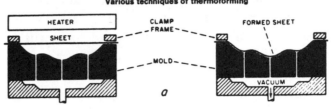

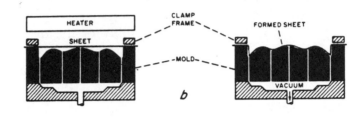

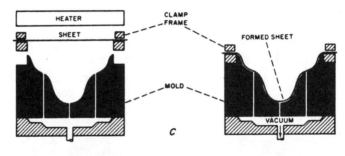

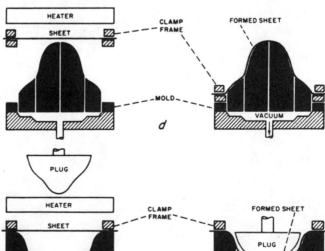

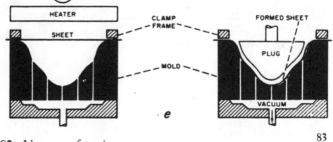

83. Vacuum forming.

Printing

The responsibilities of a good designer do not end when the artwork is released to the production personnel. To guarantee an effective job, it is the responsibility of the designer to supervise many of the steps leading to the completion of the display.

Printing is an important phase in the production of the POP display. Once the printing method is decided upon (usually lithography, flexography, or silk screen) the designer must follow through every step of the production, checking the artwork, blueprints, mechanicals, and working drawings. The designer should be available to check the job while it runs on the press, so that any variation in color and tone will be interpreted from the designer's point of view. These decisions should not be left to the pressman.

The assembly of the display is an important process: thermoforming, die cutting, stitching, gluing, stapling the display components together ready for the shipping department. To guarantee correct assembly, it is important to enclose a detailed instruction sheet with a diagram for each step of assembly.

84, 85, 86. Designer's sketches. Courtesy of Warner/Lauren, Ltd. Cosmetics.

84

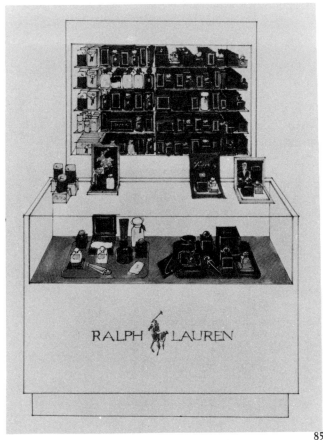

85

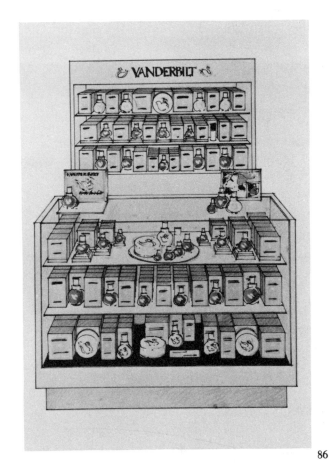

86

Project Number 1

Design a full-size display shipper to hold a variety of items in small cartons.

STEP 1: Prepare a preliminary marker sketch. Develop color, shape, copy, and a "reader." Prepare several sketches to choose from.

STEP 2: Start with a mock-up, using corrugated board or cardboard. Work out all your structural problems: folding, assembly, the shape of the reader, and the most important factor, size.

STEP 3: Build your final model. On a large tracing sheet or brown wrapping paper, draw up the pattern of the shipper. It must be a **one-piece** construction. Transfer your pattern to the board, attach or paste up finished art. Assemble display.

Project Number 2

Build a small cosmetic display tester.

STEP 1: Visit your local drugstore or department store and research this display.

STEP 2: Choose the proper merchandise — makeup items or fragrance. Prepare several marker sketches to choose from.

STEP 3: Make your mock-up. Prepare your pattern. Transfer pattern to plastic sheets (Plexiglas, styrene), cut out components, and adhere pieces with the proper adhesive (for Plexiglas, Lucite, or styrene use Rez-N-Bond or epoxy glue).

STEP 4: Use transfer types or hand lettering. For decor, use gold foil, papers in color, or cutouts adhered to the plastic. For hand lettering, use acrylic or oil colors.

Books to Read

Offenhartz, Harvey. **Point-of-Purchase Design.** N.Y, N.Y.: Van Nostrand-Reinhold, 1968.

Roth, Laszlo. **Package Design.** Englewood Cliffs, N.J.: Prentice-Hall, Inc., 1981.

Sutnar, Ladislav. **Design for Point-of-Sale.** N.Y., N.Y.: Pellegrini and Cudahy, 1952.

Publication

Creative. The Magazine of Promotion and Marketing. New York.

CHAPTER

4

Posters

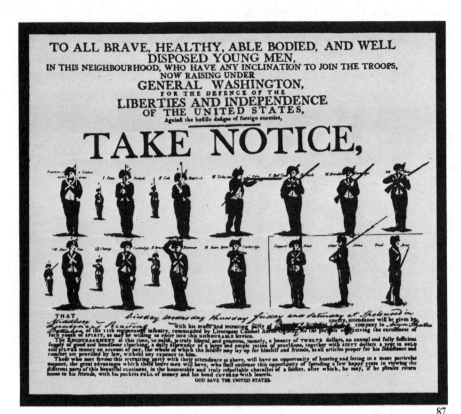

87

87. An early American recruiting poster (eighteenth century).

The printed poster has unique qualities which distinguish it from other display media. Unlike television, cinema, and printed media, the poster can leave a lasting image. Television can be turned off, the printed word can go unread, but a poster cannot be avoided. A poster can be displayed in areas other media might not reach: in remote parts of the world for illiterate societies, in foreign countries where the poster can break through the language barrier, in public vehicles where there is a captive audience, and on giant outdoor billboards above buildings.

The four basic elements of poster art are: (1) **surprise,** (2) **clarity,** (3) **drama, and** (4) **impact.** Posters sell. Whether promoting consumer products or a political candidate, a poster can inform, educate, and persuade in very specific ways. Posters criticize, satirize, and may also contain strong elements of shock. Posters come in many forms and sizes. From giant outdoor advertising billboards to tiny postage stamps, the poster fulfills the same function: It permits the viewer great latitude in interpreting and understanding a message.

88. Seventeenth century English printed notice.

89. A nineteenth century American commercial poster.

90. A Parisian kiosk. Photo by author.

88

89

74

Posters come in several categories. The commercial poster introduces and sells products and services. The political or propaganda poster introduces social and political ideas and uses the graphic medium as a means of persuasion. The art poster, designed by an artist, introduces works of art exhibited in museums and galleries. The theatrical poster announces plays, shows, films, and places of entertainment.

The ancestor of the modern poster was the printed notice, an announcement or advertisement. These printed notices were displayed on walls, at crossroads, and in public squares. The ancient Romans provided poster space on their walls in a form of whitewashed rectangles. In Pompeii, archeologists have found remnants of posters painted on papyrus, "advertising" sheets, announcing public events, plays, and decrees of government.

When lithography was invented in 1793, the intention was to reproduce works of art more cheaply than by the traditional methods of wood and metal engravings. Lithography on stone uses the principle of artwork prepared by the artist direct on a flat, porous stone with oily paint or crayons. The stone absorbs the paint. After application of water on the stone, many fine color prints (or black-and-white prints) can be produced. This method is still in use by artists.

In 1833 the rotary lithographic press was invented. This made it possible to produce several large posters from zinc plates faster than from stone. Some printed sheets were as much as ten yards long.

Lithography attracted artists. It requires skill and craftsmanship to prepare and print a fine lithograph. The collaboration between artists and lithographers produced the first real full-color poster of the nineteenth century. Artists like Daumier and Toulouse-Lautrec were pioneers of this new art form. Paris became the center of the new poster art, which became so popular that laws had to be enacted to control the flow and display of posters. Most posters were stuck on the walls. The French law of 1881 regulated the placing of posters by having a stamp affixed to them.

90

Soon kiosks began to appear on the street corners of Paris. The kiosk is a tall, wide column, approximately five by fourteen feet, with a dome, especially erected for the purpose of displaying posters on important corners of streets and avenues. It soon became a public meeting place, a sort of street-corner gallery. Other European cities adopted the kiosk. Strangely, it never caught on in America.

The commercial poster is still a powerful medium of introducing and selling products and services. After the First World War the great technological changes and innovations in transportation brought new highways, low-cost gasoline, the popular-sized automobile, buses, trains, ocean liners, and the airplane. People traveled more and more often, not only in the United States

91

92

but in Europe and in other parts of the world.

The travel poster played an important part in creating a new mobile society. Railroads, giant ocean liners, and airlines were competing with each other, using the travel poster as an advertising medium. Before the age of television, the poster introduced new commercial products and services. Posters were displayed on trains, buses, and subways.

The billboard was a very special poster erected along the busy highways. These giant posters were assembled from twenty-four separate printed sheets or painted on large panels, section by section. Graphically, the billboards had to attract potential consumers speeding by at sixty miles per hour. These giant posters later came to be regarded by concerned citizens and environmentalists as safety hazards and a public nuisance.

93. James Montgomery Flagg U.S. World War I recruiting poster.

94. Posterization. Line conversion technique by Joel A. Levirne/ Graphic Images, Ltd., New York.

The strongest poster medium is a social-political poster. Dramatic, bold, often shocking, it plays an important part in our history. One of the fine examples is the famous James Montgomery Flagg World War I recruiting poster of Uncle Sam saying "I Want You!" The Russian revolution after the First World War influenced some striking posters. The political poster has particularly flourished during and since World War II. In the United States posters for political candidates were introduced with strong emphasis on copy and photography. In Europe, striking graphics, humor, and typographic design were favored by designers. In recent years antiwar posters and posters for social changes have been the most powerful works of art. Wars, revolutions, and social changes have produced some striking, dramatic posters all over the world.

Some of the most important innovations in poster design are made by artists, for very special occasions. Examples of these are the gallery posters announcing the opening of an artist's show. Most of these posters are

93

I WANT YOU
FOR U.S.ARMY
NEAREST RECRUITING STATION

signed by the artist and printed in limited editions. Signed posters by Picasso, Calder, and Miró are expensive and valuable additions to graphic art collections.

The entertainment world has produced some fine posters. From the nineteenth-century music halls portrayed by Toulouse-Lautrec, to the movie posters of Chaplin or the Marx Brothers, many theatrical posters are now collector's items.

The art technique of the poster is no longer restricted to lithography. The poster is the cheapest and most effective advertising and display medium. Advertising agencies often use a full-page ad in a form of a poster. The poster is an integral part of a point-of-purchase display. An individual poster mounted on board, small or large, is a very effective display. Unmounted posters are often used where other displays cannot be set up, for example, on store windows and walls in supermarkets and drugstores.

One of the great advantages of the poster is that it can be produced cheaply. For

94

limited runs in full color, the silk-screen process is most economical. For a limited budget, one- or two-color offset lithography is most suitable. To keep the costs of printing plates down, poster designers developed a very special art technique: **posterization.** Posterization methods make art and illustration feasible without expensive halftones. This can be accomplished with art reproduced in line, dry brush, line conversion, and solarization.

Art in line is a simple medium of line and mass without

halftones. It is often very effective in a flat collage form, or with paste-ups or cutouts.

Dry-brush technique is well known to most designers. It consists of brush strokes on textured paper. The effect can be duplicated very successfully with crayons or spatter.

Line conversion. A mechanical system where halftone art (photos) can be converted into a line rendering or other type of line art utilizing screen patterns. A very inexpensive version of this method is achieved when a photostat or photocopy is made of a photograph; halftones tend to become solid areas.

95

95, 96, 97. Posterization. Line conversion technique by Joel A. Levirne/Graphic Images, Ltd., New York.

96

Solarization. A controlled photographic method of overexposing film to produce striking graphic images, often without halftones. This is a highly creative and experimental method for full-color reproduction.

The quality and impact of your poster does not depend on the quantity of colors. It depends on the quality of art and the careful planning of its execution. Often a two-color job in line or flat colors is more effective than a full-color one. Some of the best posters were done in black and white. It takes a designer with imagination and design sense to develop a poster with an impact. Your client's budget should always be the determining factor of the style and medium of your poster.

Virtually all art media are being used in posters today: photography, typography, traditional art, cartoons, art nouveau, art deco, pop and op styles, used singly or in combination.

Poster art is flourishing all over the world. The popularity of the poster has insured its rapid commercialization. The sale of posters directly to the public has become an important business.

Here is a gallery of posters past and present.

98

98. Henri Toulouse-Lautrec's color lithograph. From the author's collection.

99. Chaplin movie poster. From the author's collection. [Copyright © by Universal Pictures, a Division of Universal City Studios, Inc.] [Courtesy of MCA Publishing, a Division of MCA Communications, Inc.]

100. Marx Brothers movie poster. From the author's collection. [Copyright © by Universal Pictures, a Division of Universal City Studios, Inc.] [Courtesy of MCA Publishing, a Division of MCA Communications, Inc.]

101, 102. Courtesy of Seymour Chwast, designer.

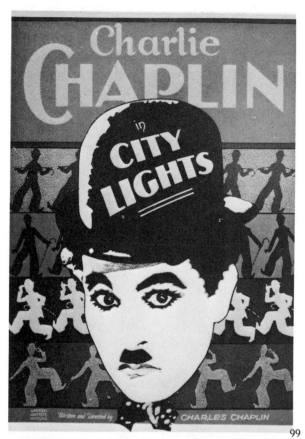

99

101

100

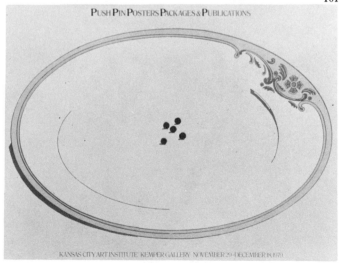

KANSAS CITY ART INSTITUTE · KEMPER GALLERY · NOVEMBER 29–DECEMBER 19, 1970

102

103, 104. Courtesy of Seymour Chwast, designer.

105. The American Ballet Theater, by Audrey Sanchez, F.I.T. student.

106. Traditional Spanish bullfight poster. From the author's collection.

107. Poster for a toy company. Courtesy of Creative Display, Inc.

103

104

105

106

107

85

108. Arthritis Foundation by Peter Jensen, F.I.T. student.

108

Project Number 1

Design a poster to bring attention to an important public issue: toxic waste or environmental protection. The poster should be in full color, executed in your best medium and technique. It must be dramatic, with a strong visual impact.

Project Number 2

Select a play, a new film, or a television program, and design a poster for it in just two colors or black and white. Posters should be prepared on illustration board. Size: 20 by 30 inches.

Books to Look at and Read

Graphis Magazine Poster Annuals. These are the finest collections of posters from all over the world. Available in your library or from Visual Communication Books, Hastings House Publishers, 10 East 40th Street, New York, N.Y. 10016.

Rossi, Attilio. **Posters.** London, New York: The Hamlyn Publishing Group Ltd., 1969.

CHAPTER

5

"SPECTACULAR!"
"HAWAII"
"IS AN ACHIEVEMENT
OF MIGHTY PROPORTIONS!"
JULIE ANDREWS
MAX VON SYDOW
RICHARD HARRIS
WESTCL
ADDIO
PALACE
PALACE

Signs and Signage

Historical background

Signs through the ages

Trade cards, handbills, and sandwich boards

Trademarks, brand names, and logos

Heraldry

The art of corporate identity

The design process of a logo

Signage for films and television

Creating titles

Exterior and interior signs

The variety of electric outdoor signs

Neon advertising signs

Signage systems

International signage

Traffic and road signs

Color studies for signage

Some unusual examples of outstanding signs

During the excavations of Pompeii and Herculaneum, archeologists found remnants of metal trade signs forged by Roman blacksmiths. Some traces of hand-painted signs were also found over the entrances to shops.

In Europe during the Middle Ages, with a highly illiterate society, obvious symbols of the particular trade were used. These were actual replicas of products or services of the trade or painted signboards with decorative metal brackets.

Some of these signs grew larger and more elaborate and projected farther out than neighboring tradesmen's signs. A civic commission was established to limit the size and projection of the trade sign, to keep the narrow street from being completely darkened. One ruling of the commission was that the sign must be placed high enough so that a man in full armor on a horse could pass beneath it.

During the fifteenth and sixteenth centuries, in most parts of Europe and in the New World, building and street numbers were adapted and the use of oversized signs and signboards declined. Some of the classic signs are still with us today: The barber pole, the three golden balls of the Medici family (used over pawnshops), and the painted and hand-carved American inn signs are often historical replicas from England and Europe. The illustrations show some of the trade signs of this period.

109

109. Carved European trade sign, seventeenth century.

110. Iron trade sign, European eighteenth century.

111. Carved European trade sign, seventeenth century.

112, 113, 114, 115. Contemporary trade signs by George Wybenga.

116. The golden balls of the Medici family: pawnshop. Photo by author.

113

114

115

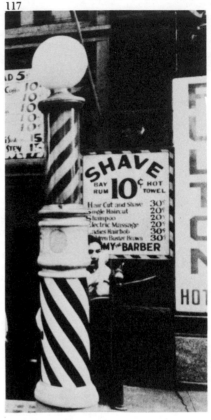

Designing and executing trade signs was considered a serious and profitable art. William Hogarth, a famous eighteenth-century English painter and engraver, originally started his career as a commercial artist, designing coats of arms, shopkeepers' signs, tradesman cards, and formal invitations for sprees and funerals.

Another curious, often intricate form of sign in metal is the weathervane. In the days of sailing ships, wind and weather were important topics. Weathervanes were usually made of copper or iron. Roosters, birds, cattle, and fish were popular subjects in rural areas. Strange beasts or tradesmen (blacksmiths, carpenters) were often represented on a weathervane.

Trade signs are with us virtually from the cradle to the grave. For centuries it was customary to mark a grave with headstones bearing elaborate carvings of images and decorative designs of cherubs, skulls, and faces. Even on the simplest stone the lettering is often beautifully proportioned and cut with great skill. Illustrated are some outstanding examples of this art.

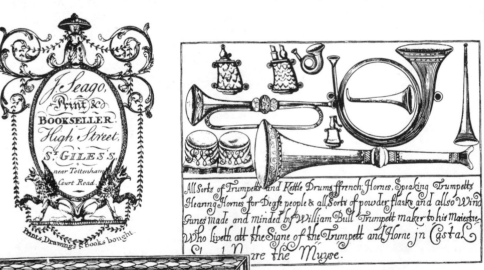

Jeane Tempell. Chimbley:
Swepers at the Signe of the woman :
Chimbley Sweper in Nutners ſtreet :
near the watch houſe in Holborn

117. The barber pole.

118. English trade cards, eighteenth century.

119. American weathervane, nineteenth century.

120. New England gravestone rubbing, nineteenth century.

120

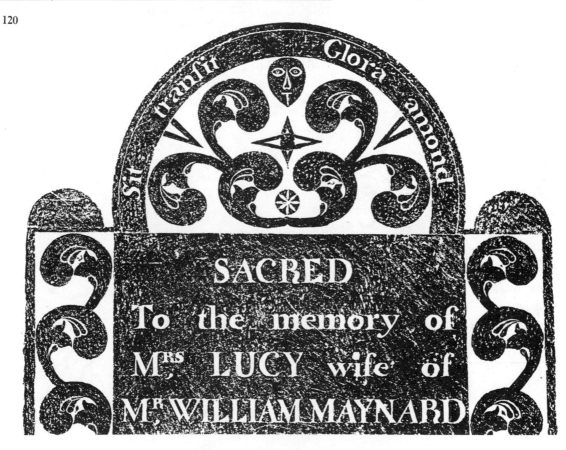

Sit transit Gloria amond

SACRED
To the memory of
M^{RS} LUCY wife of
MR WILLIAM MAYNARD

Trade Cards, Handbills, and Sandwich Boards

These fascinating forms of art were the forerunners of the present-day business card and sales promotional materials. Trade cards carried the name of the shop, with the type of goods sold, and often a reproduction of the shop sign as well. Many of the trade cards are delicate engravings with an ornamental border, the cartouche. The little round watch papers used inside watch cases, carrying the maker's name and address, were another special form of trade card.

Handbills were small, posterlike printed sheets given away at fairs, political conventions, and circuses. Other handbills were public announcements for sailing ships or steamships, railway or coach services.

Trade cards and handbills relied on decorative lettering for much of their appeal. The exuberant love of ornamental lettering of this period had a great influence on type designers. New type faces, especially display types, were originated. Most of them are still being used today (for example, Playbill, Ornées, Profil, and Wood type faces, among others).

Letters took on fantastic shapes. Illustrated are some historical examples of the display type.

Sandwich boards were carried by men on busy streets. They advertised services, merchandise, and often political and religious issues.

Iohn Wildblood at the Rainbow & 3 pidgons in St Clements Lane In Lombard Street London who Married the Widdow Harrinton Silk Dyer

121

POLLOCK'S CHARACTERS IN THE FORTY THIEVES. *Plate 8.*

Attendants.   Selim.   Hassarac.   Demon of War.

Abdalla.

Orcobrand.   Officer.   Robber.   Officer.   Robber.

London. Published by B.Pollock. 73.Hoxton Street. Hoxton

122

MONTGOMERY WARD AND COMPANY'S
CATALOGUE, SPRING AND SUMMER 1895

121. Eighteenth century decorative
alphabet (German).

122. Characters for a toy theater
play, England, nineteenth century.

123. American mail-order catalog
illustrations, 1895.

124. Decorative type and numbers,
nineteenth century.

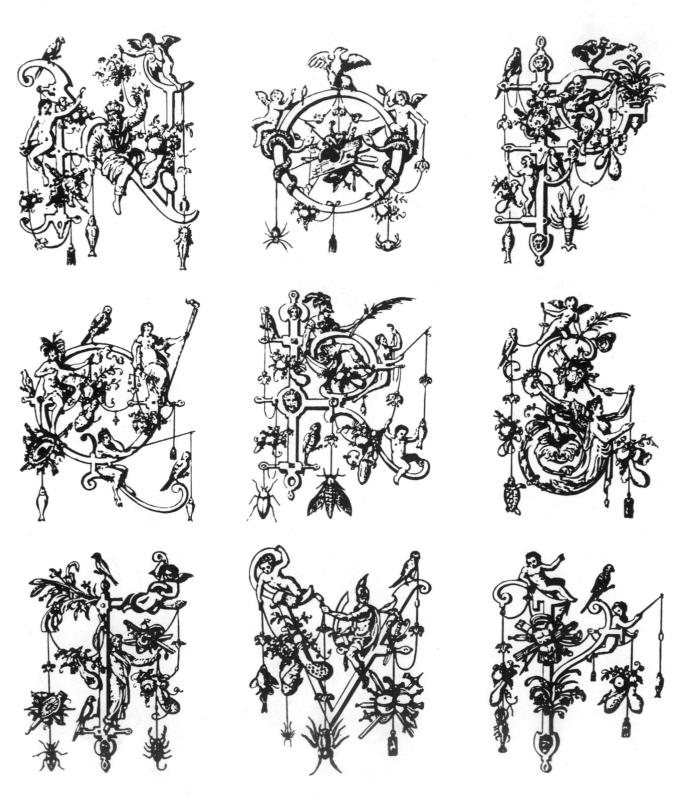

Trademarks, Brand Names, and Logos: Historical Background

Since the beginning of time, man has communicated with visual symbols. The earliest artifacts found in different parts of the world, of a wide variety of cultures, were decorated with symbols. Primitive men ruled by emotion and by their loyalty to their tribe or family. Once they established an emotional relationship with a symbol, they remained loyal to their choice.

Judaism, Christianity, Buddhism, and Muhammadanism have their distinctive symbols, since most religions forbade the making and worshipping of idols. Symbols fulfill a deep human need and symbolize universal forces of a higher being.

One of the earliest trademarks in European history was the coat of arms. In Europe during the Middle Ages and the Renaissance, **heraldry** was developed into a fine art. Coats of arms were designed for kings, knights, and noblemen. This symbol appeared on shields, rings, seals, and eventually on banners. When principalities and states were created, the coat of arms and the banner (the national flag) became the symbol of the particular state.

Some of the great artists of the Renaissance created coats of arms. While in the service of the Duke of Milan, Leonardo da Vinci designed costumes and arms, organized festivals, and supplied the court with an artistic background. His famous notebooks contain pages of designs for banners, seals, and other heraldic designs which can be called the distinctive trademarks of the period.

126

Modern Trademarks, Brand Names, and Logos: The Art of Corporate Identity

Definitions

Trademark. A graphic symbol, word, image, or letters used by the manufacturer (or service). Registered and protected by the law (TM).

Brand Names. An identification of the product by its own name, usually displayed on the package, often on the product itself.

Logo. A graphic concept of letters, forms, and/or symbols. Often consists of the name of the manufacturer (or service).

In the early 1800s manufacturers of various consumer products began to supply store fixtures marked with their signs. It was considered quite prestigious to display these items in the store. At about the same time, brand names began to appear on barrels, crates, boxes, tins, and glasses, and often on the merchandise itself. Manufacturers began to develop their own logos.

The 1800s were the most creative period in American product development and business. The style of trademarks, brand names, and logos reflect the strong Victorian tastes of the period. Some of the most outstanding products and services were originated: Kellogg, 1895; C. W. Post, 1895; Quaker Oats, 1870; Heinz 57 Varieties, 1876; A & P, 1880; Borden, 1857; Coca Cola, 1886; Ivory Soap, 1878; Gillette, 1895; Kodak, 1888; and Jell-O, 1897. By the beginning of the twentieth century names like Ford (1903) and Chevrolet (1911) became household words, and their trademarks were recognized all over the world.

By the end of the nineteenth century thousands of new consumer-goods manufacturers were formed. Laws had to be passed to register trademarks with the government. Fair competition laws were enacted by Congress to protect brand names.

In our own time a new graphic medium has emerged: the art of corporate identity, twentieth century corporate coat of arms. By 1976 trademark encyclopedias listed over three thousand logotypes and trademarks of importance (not to mention small companies, which emerge practically every day; they, too, have their own corporate identity.)

127

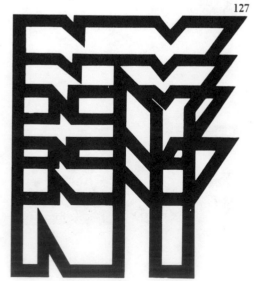

127. Logos for New York City. By the author.

128. Concepts for corporate identity by Mitchell Gottlieb, F.I.T. student.

129. Logos, corporate identities, and trademarks by F.I.T. students.

129

130. Signage for the 1976 Olympic Games in Montreal, Canada. Design by Hunter, Straker, Templeton, Ltd. Courtesy of Bicultural Information Committee of Public Words, Canada.

Today, in the corporate world, the trademark — whether used by a single firm or a large group, for a product or for a specific service — has become a symbol of quality. By associating its name or trademark with a product, the maker is offering a guarantee of quality.

A picture of a graphic symbol is universal. A logo or trademark must have the international language to be identified by any observer with the appropriate word in his own language. The methodologies of creating corporate-identity symbols vary with designers. Some designers get good results by starting with the natural shape of the object, or "the essence of things." Others begin with a simple form and enrich it with individual features until it can stand on its own. Absolute simplicity is not always the best solution. The design must be unique and timeless, a sort of visual shorthand like those of many cultures in the past, who have designed magnificent signs and symbols on pottery, fabrics, and carvings. Here are some of the successful logos, brand names, and trademarks by contemporary designers from all over the world.

Signage for Films and Television

Motion pictures and television have changed our way of entertainment, as well as stimulated and influenced the arts, sciences, and education. What is more important, these media have brought millions of people together. TV educates, entertains, and introduces and sells new products. On videotape, we can view feature films and sports events; we can also learn new skills **at home** whenever we choose. We have slide presentations and a wide variety of audiovisual techniques to present and sell products. The designer plays an important part in these mass-communication systems. It is the designer who produces storyboards, animation, costumes, sets,

and above all, the signage and titles for these media. Typography, handlettering, and drawing are essential for the designer.

Long before television, movie titles were given great attention by directors and producers. Most movie titles consisted of artwork combined with hand lettering. Not until the advent of television did the title become an all-important vehicle for the film. By the 1960s animation and special effects produced by computers were being used for titles. The combination of the computer and the imagination of the designer has produced remarkable, often shocking, effects in signage as well as in animation.

The title is a sort of book jacket. Essentially, it is informative. It tells you the title of the film or show, and it lists the names of actors, technicians, the director, and the producer. Signage is often combined with animated or still backgrounds, or simply superimposed onto the film itself. The viewer is attracted to the striking graphic images and, like a book jacket or a magazine cover, these images appeal to our aesthetic sense as well as to our emotions.

As time goes on, styles change. This applies to titles, too. In recent years major feature films have used simple typographic titles, whereas television

131

often relies on shocking and colorful computer-devised titles. Television is a fast, competitive medium, with "the hand on the dial." Titles must hold the attention of the viewer.

Title design is part of the work of the TV, film, and slide-presentation graphic designer. To break into this creative, well-paid field, the designer must have an interesting portfolio of hand lettering, type, logos, and corporate-identity graphics. The designer must be familiar with basic animation techniques, including the principles of computer graphics. The following pages contain excellent examples that may help you to develop your talent.

131. Signage for television (experimental) by Lisa Grabowski.

132, 133. Television titles by the author.

132

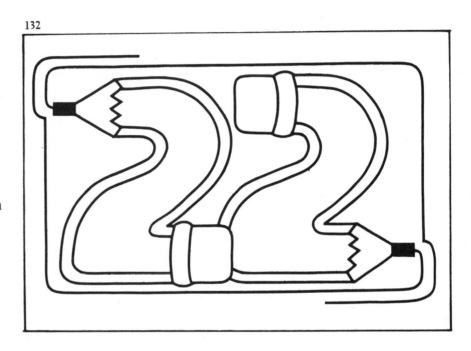

133

134. Television titles by the author.

135. Movie title. By the author.

136. Outdoor metal sign. Courtesy of Mobil Oil Corporation.

Exterior and Interior Signs

The earliest illuminated signs were constructed over theater marquees during the gaslight era. Sheet-metal plates with cutout openings that represented lettering or designs, backed with colored glass lenses, were used in front of gas jets, which were lighted every night. The effects were rather attractive, somewhat similar to electric light.

After Thomas Edison invented his first successful carbon lamp in 1879, inventors and promoters tried for years to utilize this new, brilliant source of light for an outdoor sign. By 1900 the first electric sign was erected in New York City. It was six stories high and ablaze with 1,200 electric light bulbs, advertising Heinz 57 Varieties. The "world's largest pickle" was made out of hundreds of electric lights!

It did not take long to realize the importance of this brand new advertising medium, and New York City's Broadway was soon called "The Great White Way." The use of electrical outdoor signs has become so widespread that many buildings are erected with supports and fixtures to which signs can be attached.

The first electrical motion effects were produced by motor-driven electric contacts or switches. These signs are called **flashers.** In some electric signs, circuits are arranged so that some of the lights are off while others are on. Some signs can display a variety of animation with their brightly colored lights; others create special effects: blowing smoke, real waterfalls, and moving light copy to tell us the latest news, correct time, and temperature. Our modern, often computer-oriented signs provide the· man on the street with continual entertainment.

The first neon advertising sign was installed in 1923 on the Cosmopolitan Theater in New York City. Neon lights are made of colored gas encased in a glass tube, which can be shaped into different forms and letters. When electricity is conducted through the gas, it produces brilliant, colorful light. Neon signs are the most exciting and spectacular sights in our cities. Las Vegas and New York City are the most talked-about "neon capitals" of the world. Some of these signs are over 100 feet high, containing some 5,000 feet of neon

136

tubing and 4,370 incandescent color lights!

With the invention of the fluorescent light, fluorescent electric signs became practical for both outdoor and indoor use. Fluorescent tubes inside a glass or plastic casing make the sign visible from all sides.

The soft drink and liquor industries give away illuminated indoor signs for restaurants and bars. These are sometimes replicas of antiques, lamps, trademarks, clocks, and novelties; they advertise and remind the consumer of their products. Service stations use illuminated outdoor signs, and supermarkets and variety stores often display this type of sign over the storefront.

137

138

139

140

137. Large outdoor neon sign. Courtesy of Artkraft Strauss Sign Corporation.

138. Broadway signs, New York City. Courtesy of Artkraft Strauss Sign Corporation.

139. 3-D sign over Broadway, New York City. Courtesy of Artkraft Strauss Sign Corporation.

140. Painted 3-D sign, Broadway, New York City.

141. Neon sign.

141

Signage Systems: International Signage

Olympic games, trade fairs, international transportation centers, and public service signs are the most important signage projects in our multilingual, industrialized mass society.

Traffic and road signs use international symbols that can be understood by anyone, anywhere in the civilized world. Symbols or glyphs must be obvious for quick, accurate readings and interpretations. Forms must be simplified so they can be recognized by anyone. Color studies are important to develop the proper color codes for the symbol or message. White on red indicates danger, prohibition, or fire safety hazards. Warning signs are black on yellow. Information and permissive signs are white on blue. Type face or lettering is also important. In recent years Helvetica has been much favored and used by designers. Other sharp, sans serif faces make attractive and highly readable signs. Some countries and communities have realized the importance of good signage. The ideal solution to the problem of signage lies in teamwork. Town planners, architects, designers, and authorities must join forces to find the best answer to a specific need and at the same time contribute to the aesthetic improvement of the urban and country scene.

142. Road signs, USA.

142

Project Number 1

Develop your own corporate-identity symbol. This can be part of your stationary, business card, and your company's promotional material.

Start out by doing extensive typographic research. Find a suitable type face that can be converted into a logo or trademark. Begin with some small, rough pencil or Pentel sketches (thumbnails). In most schools the students must come up with seventy-five to one hundred variations. This is a design project where imagination and maximum creativity are put to test. Symmetry and proportions are important factors. A distinctive corporate identity is easy to recognize; it should be simple, graphically communicating the designer's concept of the service or the nature of the business.

It will take time to make the final decision or choice of the best logo. Remember, the logo or trademark will become a **permanent** symbol of the business.

Now that you have made the selection, you must prepare the final art. This should be done in black india ink two or three times the size you need. By working in a larger format than the final desired size, you are able to work accurately. Your curves and the openings of letters or symbols will be smooth after you reduce the logo to the proper size. A well-designed logo looks good even if it is one-half inch in size.

Project Number 2

Now that you have a logo, develop the following signage components: 1. Stationery, an envelope, and a business card. 2. Assume that you are designing signage for a retail establishment, in this case for a chic specialty store (or boutique). Design an exterior and an interior sign. The exterior sign should be made of fluorescent lights in a casing to be placed over the entrance. The interior sign should be made of neon, to be used in various places inside the store.

Once you have the logo, designing stationery is a matter of selecting the proper type face and the right paper. However, the most important decision is the layout, determining how the logo and the type will look together. This will take a lot of layout sketches in actual size. The quality of paper you use is very important. Do not choose cheap-looking novelty papers. Use only excellent quality papers. Your business card should be highly readable, especially your telephone number. Embossing is a very effective aesthetic approach for your logo only. Do not attempt to use blind embossing for small type. It is almost impossible to read blind-embossed letters on a small card. Use restraint and good taste when it comes to color. Remember — stationery conveys the image of the owner!

Designing exterior and interior signs for a boutique can be fun. Your illuminated sign will be made of plastics. Almost any style of lettering can be utilized here. The neon sign has limitations, but the effects are more dramatic. To develop the signs, you must make a sketch of the storefront and try to place the sign in its proper place. With overlays, you can create some variations. Some designers use enlarged photos (in color) of the storefront to try out a variety of overlays. For both neon signs and illuminated signs, you must have a working drawing to scale or, when possible, actual size. Visit your local sign shop and watch the exciting process of sign making.

Books to Read:

Ballinger, Louise and Raymond. **Sign, Symbol and Form.** N.Y., N.Y.: Van Nostrand, Reinhold Co., 1972.

Hornung, Clarence P. **Handbook of Designs and Devices.** N.Y., N.Y.: Dover Publications, 1946.

Hornung, Clarence P. **Handbook of Early Advertising Art,** Vols. 1 and 2. N.Y., N.Y.: Dover Publications, 1956.

Lambert, M. and Enid Marx. **English Popular Art.** London: B.T. Batsford Ltd., 1951.

Mack, Kathy. **American Neon.** N.Y., N.Y.: Universe Books, 1976.

Places to Visit

Artkraft Strauss (The world's largest sign makers)
New York, N.Y.

Your local sign maker

CHAPTER

6

Sales Environments

Nature and man-made environments for selling

Architectural and mobile selling environments

The shopping mall

Traffic-free shopping areas

Reconstructed environments

Parks, habitats, trade fairs, fashion shows

Multiple-use complexes

Mobile selling environments

Entertainment, recreational art, and educational environments

The staging of a fashion show

Multimedia and audiovisual systems

New opportunities for the talented and creative designer in the field of visual communication and merchandising

We live in a consumer-oriented society. There is a lively competition going on to convince the prospective consumer to buy a particular product or service. We use every means to keep the image of the product in front of the potential consumer. Shop windows, signage, point-of-purchase displays, and posters perform the task of presenting and promoting our everyday needs. With twentieth century technologies at hand, there is just no limit to what we can do to devise new methods in the art of visual merchandising.

For the designer, display design problems are both aesthetic and technical. In the business world, social, political, and economic considerations rather than aesthetic ones alone will determine a format and the medium of an advertising campaign or a promotion. The free-enterprise system encourages every possible means of competition in the marketplace, and man-made environments play an important part in this competition.

Our environments — land, sea, and air — are made by nature. Man also makes his own environments. He builds habitats, towns, cities, service and shopping centers, fairs, shows, and amusement parks. Man-made environments as well as nature's have been used and utilized to present and promote products, services, and social or political ideas. Leisure time, educational, and recreational facilities also play an important part in man-made environments.

Architectural Environments

Creating total environments has tempted designers since the beginning of civilization. In the fifth century B.C., the Athenian leader Pericles superintended the complete reconstruction of the Acropolis in Athens, along lines that would symbolize the noble ideals of Greek culture. The writings of the Roman architect Vitruvius were a great influence on generations of European architects.

During the Middle Ages wars ravaged Europe. Cities survived by building walls and fortifications which could be defended against enemy attacks. The gradual establishment of peace brought revival of trade and the growth of the medieval city. Central areas grew up around plazas, civic buildings, and churches. Port cities developed even faster because of the shipping trade, whereas inland cities depended on local trade. In case of an invasion they found shelter inside the secure walls of the city, one of the finest of which is Avila in Spain. The city is completely encircled with a wall.

The industrial revolution of the nineteenth century urbanized western Europe. New methods of transportation made it possible for cities to have food and raw materials from all parts of the world. New development in manufacturing methods, machines, and inventions enabled the cities to produce goods which they could trade for raw materials.

143. The Erechtheum at the Acropolis, Athens, Greece.

144. Theater at Epidaurus, Greece.

145. The walls of Avila, Spain.

146. The bazaars of Istanbul.

Shopping Centers and Malls

During the post-World War II era, one of the most fertile areas for the designer was in the American suburbs that began to spring up around the cities. The suburban shopping center was created for the suburban dweller. It provided the shopper with ample parking space and large landscaped areas. Centers (or malls) became increasingly elaborate, containing restaurants, theaters, and discos. The shopping center with its multiple stores and services is now a core for American buying patterns. Supermarkets and retailing chains are a new field for the designer.

The idea behind the traffic-free shopping area is in itself not new. In 1867, in the city of Milan, Italy, the Gallery of Victor Emmanuel was opened for the public. It consisted of two glass-covered streets, with nearly a hundred shops, restaurants, and cafés. In the United States as well as in Europe, a number of covered malls have been built in recent years in cities as well as suburbs. A fine example of this type of shopping center is New York City's Citicorp mall. An interesting variation of the shopping mall is the traffic-free pedestrian street.

147

Reconstructed Environments; Theme Parks

148

147. The Galleria Vittorio Emanuelle, Milan, Italy.

148. Central Park, New York City, designed by Frederic Law Olmstead in 1858.

149. Washington Square, New York City.

149

The opportunity to redesign or reconstruct a town or city provides the ultimate in creative possibilities. Colonial Williamsburg is a splendid example of a perfect reconstructed environment.

The first man-made park in the United States was the Boston Common, created in 1634 as a community ground. By the 1850s parks had been created in most cities. They were designed principally for quiet walks or for relaxing upon benches. During the 1900s city planners created the modern park, with all its recreational facilities for sports, boating, picnicking, concerts, and shows. The amusement park is another variety of park. Disney World and Disneyland are among the finest of this type; they are make-believe worlds designed to entertain both children and adults.

Habitats

Not all designed environments are meant for people. Under special circumstances the designer may be called upon to plan environments for animals outside their natural habitat. The San Diego Zoo and the Bronx (N.Y.) Zoo are fine examples of this type of environment. Botanical gardens like Fairchild in Miami or the New York Botanical Garden are environments for exotic trees and plants.

150. Brooklyn, New York, Botanical Garden.

151. Buckminster Fuller geodesic dome.

150

Trade Fairs

The most remarkable man-made environment of our times is the international trade fair (often called a world's fair or expo). Such fairs represent the combined efforts of architects, designers, painters, sculptors, and performers. Every aspect of trade, business, entertainment, and cultural events are represented by almost every nation in the world. Pavilions, exhibit areas, amusement parks, shows, and presentations are designed by the foremost talent of each nation. An expo is a showcase of what nations could accomplish by living together in peace and harmony. Some of the revolutionary, new environments presented for the first time in expos were Buckminster Fuller's geodesic dome (Expo '67, Montreal), inflated plastic environments, and mass-produced modular housing.

The nineteenth century World's Fair introduced the transparent building. (Sir Joseph Paxton's Crystal Palace of 1851). Some recent transparent designs include mirrored buildings. These are transparent only at night, when inside lights are on.

151

Multiple-use Complexes

The technical ability of the architect to enclose enormous spaces may lead to the design of total communities in a single structure. Architects Le Corbusier and Frank Lloyd Wright were pioneers in the conception of this type of environment. Their ideas for huge hotels, apartment and office complexes, shopping and entertainment centers, industrial parks, resorts, and academic centers are today becoming structural facts.

Architectural environments affect people beyond the focus of awareness. They are symbols of man's great capacity to create and present new ideas and to improve the quality of living for millions.

Mobile Selling Environments

The designer plays an important part in all man-made environments. It is the designer who develops the visual concept of the environment, whether it is architectural or mobile.

The first commercial vehicle that sold products in America must have belonged to the itinerant peddler. His covered wagon, filled with manufactured goods, traveled the unknown, unsafe West, often pursued by Indians and unfriendly settlers. The peddler was inventive, well aware of the power of display. His wagon was a moving shop window, full of wares. It contained pots and pans, yard goods, patent medicines, notions, everything and anything the pioneers would need. It was a red-letter day when the peddler appeared with his wagon. The peddler and his wagon became part of the history of retailing. The founders of some of our large retail establishments were often former peddlers.

The mobile vehicle selling wares is still much a part of our life. Everyone remembers the sound of bells when the ice cream truck appeared on the street. The traditional hot dog wagon has always been part of the American scene.

In our time, young entrepreneurs in our cities and towns have developed a number of service vehicles. There are those that cater exotic food and beverages, complete lunches, health food, and many other categories. The old pushcart market is being revived by hundreds of eager merchants. It is conceivable that the mobile store or service of the future may compete with the shopping center by visiting the home of the suburban dweller and selling direct to the consumer.

In the health and educational field, mobile services are numerous. Most communities maintain mobile diagnostic clinics to test and educate the population. Crime- and fire-prevention units are operated by the local police and fire departments. Mobile lending

152

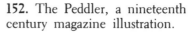

153

155

156

157

libraries are provided by public library systems. There are mobile theater units in our larger cities. It would be inconceivable to imagine an election without the traditional bandwagon, equipped with loudspeakers and bright signs to extoll the virtues of the candidate. Huge trailer trucks and cabs are fast-moving billboards. The Goodyear blimp is a familiar sight to most of us. Skywriting and hot-air balloons represent the new heights that have been reached in advertising.

The finest and the most spectacular mobile display is the float. Everyone loves a parade, and floats play an important part in the parade. Holiday celebrations and sport events use clever, imaginative floats. Some of the most exciting floats are presented in the annual Thanksgiving Day parade by New York's Macy's department store. Thousands of people, young and old, line the avenues to watch this colorful show, a moving display that introduces, sells, and promotes products and services.

Mobile rides and small carnivals provide a variety of entertainment for all ages. The circus parade is part of the American scene.

158

159

160

158. Service station. Courtesy of Mobil Oil Corporation.

159. Mobile selling environment. Courtesy of Federal Express Corporation.

160, 161, 162. Macy's Thanksgiving Day parade float. Courtesy of Macy's, New York City.

161

162

Entertainment, Fashion, Art, and Educational Environments

163

164

The electronic age gave birth to an exciting environment: the disco (short for discothèque). This exciting environment evolved from the fine-art world of the 1960s, from the world of optical, kinetic, and pop art, and from the "happenings," an environmental art form that is a realistic replica of time, place, and sound. This special environment of sound (music), light, and color is an explosive, exciting force in our contemporary culture. It is an environment that completely stimulates the senses and creates a state of excitement and fun. The spirit of disco found its way into the small boutique shops, often located within a large department store or shopping mall. Merchandise becomes chic and contemporary in the boutique environment; the boutique generates an attitude of being fashionable.

Selling fashions and accessories is another major task for the designer. Fashion shows are veritable show business productions. Buyers of fashions come from all over the world to look at new styles. The success of the fashion business depends on the presentation. It takes a very special designer, one with a *feel* for fashion and with an understanding of the change of styles and taste, to design and stage a successful fashion show.

It takes many experts to design and stage the show, including attractive models, makeup artists, hair stylists, lighting experts, fashion coordinators, and of course the display artist who designs the environment of the presentation, usually in a theaterlike atmosphere. Color, lighting, and music all play an important part in the presentation. The models walk toward the audience while an announcer describes their clothing. The show must have precision and timing. In-store fashion shows are more casual;

163, 164. The Red Parrot Disco. Photo by Bob Rich.

165. Stadium score board. Courtesy of Artkraft Strauss Sign Corporation.

166. The Givenchy fashion show at the Fashion Institute of Technology.

165

166

167. The Givenchy fashion show at the Fashion Institute of Technology.

168, 169. The Mariano Fortuny fashion fabric show. Courtesy of the Edward C. Blum Design Laboratory, Fashion Institute of Technology.

170. Design education, Pratt Institute. Designer: Etan Manasse, Etan Manasse Associates, Inc.

167

169

168

however, it takes a designer with great fashion flair to stage a successful show in the store for customers and on stage for buyers.

Most designers are familiar with 35 mm slides and filmstrips. The projection of multiple images with sound is a remarkable medium that can sell merchandise, present new concepts, and educate people.

The origins of **multimedia** can be traced to Moholy-Nagy (one of the founders of the Bauhaus movement) and his concepts of visual education and expression. His studies in painting, sculpture, and kinetics formed the basis of

some of today's visual communications. He envisaged the **participation** of the spectator in environmental spectacles. The part-theatrical activity of the happening involves the spectator in an experience that extends in time as well as in space. It uses all materials and media: sounds, motions, even smells are all in continuous space involving the spectator.

Technically, today's multimedia system is a simple one. Several projectors operate at the same time and are synchronized with sound. Each slide module is several feet square, and usually two to four modules are

presented at the same time. The impact on the viewer can be very strong, as images practically surround him or her, often creating a subliminal experience. The outgrowth of this medium is the commercial Cinerama and various 3-D projection systems. Multimedia and its simpler version, the audiovisual system, are important methods for POP display presentations, and are invaluable systems for exhibits. There are portable models of audiovisual units, most suitable for sales presentations. Both multimedia and audiovisual systems are the creations of imaginative designers with a definite flair for the theatrical.

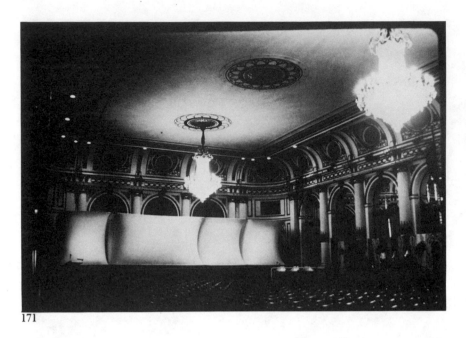

171

171. American Broadcasting
Company multimedia. Designer:
Etan Manasse, Etan Manasse
Associates, Inc.

172, 173, 174, 175. Modular office
furniture by the author.

In the 1930s the American
sculptor Alexander Calder
created a new art form,
mobiles, which successfully
integrated motion into
sculpture. Calder's mobiles
were quickly adapted for
commercial use, particularly
in the point-of-purchase
area. The mobile is still the
most effective and
inexpensive way of
presenting advertising images
and messages. Other
balancing devices followed
the mobile, all based on
natural kinetics.

Today we are utilizing every
aspect of the natural as well
as the man-made
environment to sell and
promote products and
services. One of the earliest
recorded promotions using
the natural environment

dates back to ancient
Greece. People on public
beaches wore sandals with
metal engravings of their
names or messages on the
soles. Wherever they walked,
the name or the message
was imprinted on the wet
sand. The Trojan horse, the
Colossus of Rhodes, and the
famous lighthouse of
Alexandria all prove that
man used every means to
promote an idea or a
product.

The Romans were natural
promoters. To commemorate
victories they erected
triumphal arches and
displayed elaborate fireworks;
banners and emblems added
color to their parades and
public displays. The
Christian era devoted most
of the visual aspect of art to
religion and the preservation
of faith. Churches and holy
places (environments) were
all in the service of religion.
Not until the industrial age
were visual promotions put
into service for business and
commerce.

Visual merchandising
reached its highest point in
recent years when designers
rediscovered the label on our
garments and accessories. It
is now prestigious to display
labels prominently on the
outside of the garment.

132

172

173

174

175

T-shirts and jeans advertise brand names, products, services, and even political or religious messages. This great idea is clearly the brainchild of a clever designer. The outside display of brand names is well accepted on other products like cars, sporting equipment, and accessories (scarves, handbags, luggage). We have now a new kind of designer, one who is not only aware of trends, but who *invents* new ones and uses these for a marketing and merchandising advantage.

This chapter demonstrates again the endless opportunities waiting for you in the field of visual communications and merchandising. No other field will offer so much freedom and versatility to the designer. It takes a designer with skill and imagination to be successful in this field. Test yourself with the following project:

Project: Model for a Children's Playground

This is a project that requires careful preparation, planning, design, and execution. You will construct a scale model of a children's playground.

The first step is to prepare some idea sketches, drawings, and detailed plans. The playground is for small children (preschool age). It should contain a lot of play equipment: swings, sandbox,

133

slides, a playhouse on stilts, monkey bars, a small pool, and other playthings children would enjoy.

Once your idea sketches have been developed, it is necessary to prepare work drawings of all components on scale one foot to one-half inch. Now the work drawings must be made into patterns to construct the various playthings. I recommend styrene for constructions, because it can be bent, rolled, and bonded with Rez-N-Bond.® It will set almost instantly. Balsa wood, cardboard, tubes, and rods can be utilized for various effects.

The grounds must be developed; trees, shrubs, and paths must be added. Use a lot of natural materials such as stones, small gravel, sand, and twigs for trees. When completed, the entire project should be photographed from different angles (Kodak Ektachrome 35 mm slides are recommended). Cutout figures of children playing would add to the appearance and quality of this fine model.

Books to Read

Bell, Daniel. **Toward the Year 2000: Work in Progress.** Boston: Beacon Press, 1969.

Feldman, Edmund Burke. **Varieties of Visual Experiences,** 2nd Ed. Englewood Cliffs, N.J.: Prentice-Hall, Harry N. Abrams, 1981.

Hombeck, James S. **Stores and Shopping Centers.** N.Y., N.Y.: McGraw Hill Book Co., 1962.

Nelson, George. **How to See.** Boston: Little, Brown & Co., 1977.

CHAPTER

7

Exhibit Design

The word **exhibit,** according to the dictionary, means: "To offer, to expose, to view, to manifest or display, to present something to public view." Unlike the point-of-purchase display, the exhibit does not sell, it introduces. The successful exhibit is creative marketing in three dimensions, using art, science, traffic patterns, colors, graphics, lighting, and audiovisual presentations to attract an audience, the prospective buyer or consumer of the company's products or services. From giant world's fairs and trade shows to a small gallery of works of art, exhibits present, inform, educate, and entertain.

Exhibits, expositions, and fairs were held in ancient times. The occasion was a public event. We have recorded historical evidence of the Phoenicians' fairs (about 1000 B.C.), where trading goods were exhibited and sold to the public. The fairs of ancient Greece were held along with festivals honoring the gods. The famous Olympic games comprised such a fair. In ancient Rome there was a yearly festival in April in honor of Jupiter.

One of the most famous fairs was recorded by Marco

Polo in the late 1200s. The fair was held at Kinsai, China's great capital city, which was ruled by Kublai Khan. Kinsai was the trade center of China. Its fairs took place in ten great squares in a four-mile area. Half a million visitors came to see the fair of Kinsai. The variety of goods, as Marco Polo described them, were beyond the imagination of Europeans of that time.

Most European fairs were held in honor of Christian saints. The fairs held in large cities became important trade centers.

The first important international exposition was held in London in 1851. The exposition was housed in a giant glass structure, the Crystal Palace. It attracted more than six million visitors from all over the world. There were fifteen thousand exhibitors, and among the main exhibits were the McCormick reaper and the Colt repeating pistol.

Other expositions followed. The New York Crystal Palace Exhibition of 1853–54 featured the first passenger elevator and the sewing machine. The Centennial Exposition in Philadelphia in 1876 honored Alexander Graham Bell for his

telephone. At the World's Columbian Exposition in Chicago in 1893, structural steel and electricity were featured. Expositions since the 1800s have presented new technical and scientific developments. International expositions (Expos) at St. Louis, New York, Brussels, and Montreal were important events.

Not all expositions have the scope of an international fair. Trade associations sponsor shows in our large cities all over the country. New York City, Chicago, Boston, Los Angeles, Atlanta, New Orleans, Dallas, and Houston are some of the principal trade show cities in the United States.

To illustrate the importance of the trade show business in the United States, the Trade Show Bureau's statistics on the trade show industry published the following facts and information: In 1979 U.S. business spent $5,943,000 to exhibit in 7,857 trade shows. An additional $7,454,000 was spent by 29,350,000 trade show attendees for travel, hotels, meals, and entertainment. Trade shows are big business, and the designer plays an important part in this giant enterprise.

176. Centennial (1876) Exposition in Philadelphia (contemporary print).

177. New York World's Fair, 1964–65. Photo by Bob Golby.

177

Exhibit design requires the training of a graphic designer, a structural designer, an architect, and a display-interior designer. Exhibit design is truly a three-dimensional experience. It is probably one of the most creative and versatile crafts.

There are basically two separate exhibit systems. The first is the ready-made exhibit, which consists of stock or prefabricated packaged units developed, designed, and distributed by special firms. There are several categories of this type of exhibit units: modular, pole systems, panels, tubular, and others.

A modest modular system kit six feet high and three feet wide, with three panels, shelf, and pedestal made of Fome-Cor can cost as little as $150.* Readymade exhibits are designed to present a wide variety of merchandise and services. Some of the important features are portability; fast assembly, often without specific tools; and packageability for shipping and storage. (There is a list of manufacturers and distributors of ready-made

*Prices are subject to change, of course.

exhibits at the end of this chapter.)

The second type of exhibit is the custom exhibit, designed for individual need, which provides complete freedom in design and material selection. The cost of a custom exhibit varies depending on size, materials, and design. A modest ten-foot exhibit shouldn't cost more than $3,000–$4,000, but a complex, large exhibit can cost as much as $100,000!

Large national and international corporations with a unique story to tell at a trade show usually have a custom exhibit as an important communication and marketing tool.

In the past, the standard exhibit was a large architectural unit. Contemporary exhibit designers now use new, lightweight materials, new techniques of transportation and installation in the exhibit hall. Designers are stressing flexibility, modularity, and portability to keep custom exhibits economical and to make them more versatile and useful.

Some of the new materials used are lightweight plastics,

foams, fabrics, Fiberglas, aluminum, and a variety of lightweight panels made of such things as Fome-Cor, honeycomb, stretched fabric panels, and decorative papers and boards. Some exhibit design organizations specialize in specific types of designs and/or special facilities for audiovisual presentations, animations, or multimedia. Other companies are specialists in a particular industry such as medicine, health, publishing, or the food industry. The success of a trade show is ultimately based on the partnership between the exhibitor and the designer, which creates a selling environment that is attractive, impressive, and effective.

The Design Process of an Exhibit

The first step in exhibit design starts with the selection of an exhibit plan or theme that will promote the company's message and products at the trade show. The important question is, "Why are you going into this exhibit and what do you hope to get out of it?"

Exhibitors with specific trade-show objectives are most likely to place a premium on a creative, marketing-oriented exhibit design to introduce products or services and to produce **sales leads.**

All forms of communication tools and techniques can be used to attract attention and tell a story at a trade show. Live demonstrations of new products, especially those that involve the show visitor, are among the most effective forms of demonstration. Animation, transparencies, photographic blowups, and puppets are other excellent techniques.

Audiovisual presentations are one of the most effective systems introducing products and services. One of the recent developments of this

medium is the **touch-sensitive screen.** Touching a picture, a word, or a symbol on the screen creates informative new pictures, sequences, words, and diagrams. The technology is called the interactive videodisc: the symbiosis of the computer and the laser-vision disc.

This informative and educational system was set up in the United States Pavilion at the Energy Expo '82 (the Knoxville, Tennessee, World's Fair). Inside the pavilion there

178

179

178. The Knoxville World's Fair, 1982, the United States Pavilion. Designer: Albert H. Woods, Carlos Ramirez/Albert H. Woods, Inc.

179. The interior of the United States Pavilion. Designer: Albert H. Woods, Carlos Ramirez/Albert H. Woods, Inc.

were 42 TV screens connected to 42 videodisc machines, which were hooked up to 23 Apple II computers. This system allowed 480 energy-related terms to be demonstrated and explained visually by simply touching a picture of what one wanted to understand. This system is probably the best information and educational system available today; it is especially suitable for exhibits.

The planning and organization of an exhibit should start a minimum of six months in advance. The designer's first step is to work out design objectives and strategies with the exhibitor's advertising manager or the person in charge of developing an exhibit for the company.

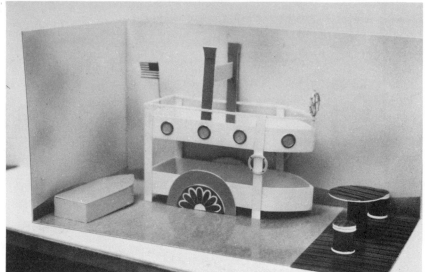

181

180

182

183

144

184

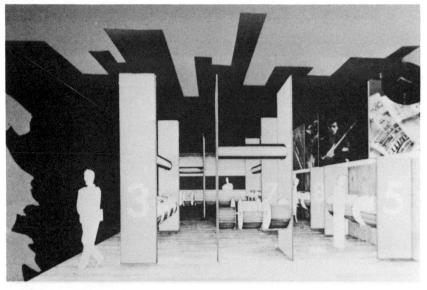

185

186

180. Modular trade show exhibit for Allied Corporation. Designer: Howard Mont, Howard Mont Associates, Inc.

181. Model for boy's room with a nautical theme by the author.

182. Model for a historical dollhouse. Courtesy of Ideal Toy Corporation.

183. Model for a set design by Orit Singer, F.I.T. student.

184. Sketch for an exhibit by Anne Strait, F.I.T. student.

185. Sketch for a store interior by Mimi Malamud, F.I.T. student.

186. The D.G. Williams mannequin showroom.

Preliminary sketches (concepts) executed in a realistic style, done in markers or tempera, and work drawings (architectural) indicating building and construction materials carry the exhibit design from its initial concept to its final form. In many cases, before the actual construction begins, the designer will develop and provide an actual scale model of the exhibit, thereby allowing the company's management to visualize the final shape and construction of the exhibit in three-dimensional form.

On the following pages you will see some noteworthy custom exhibits by outstanding designers which have been used recently.

187. International Communications Agency, Washington, D.C. Designers: Etan Manasse, Etan Manasse Associates, Inc.

188. Reeves Teletype, New York City. Designer: Etan Manasse, Etan Manasse Associates, Inc.

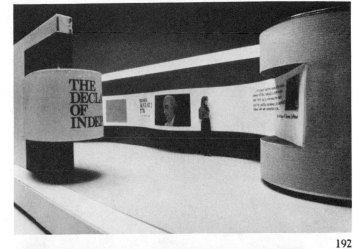

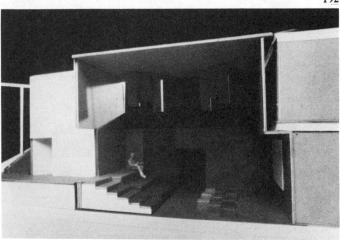

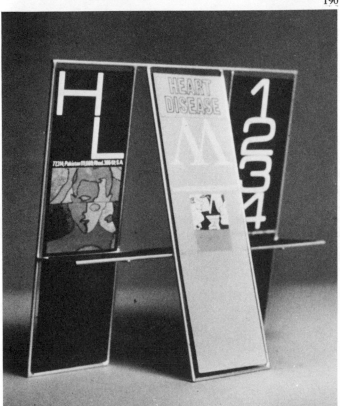

189. An aerial view of a shopping mall by an F.I.T. interior design class.

190. Traveling exhibit for Hoffman-LaRoche. Designer: Howard Mont, Howard Mont Associates, Inc.

191. Thomas Jefferson exhibit, Graff House, Philadelphia. Designer: Howard Mont, Howard Mont Associates, Inc.

192. Graff House, model of theater. Designer: Howard Mont, Howard Mont Associates, Inc.

Project: Custom Exhibit for a Manufacturer of Paint Products

Design a colorful exhibit introducing new paint products: a water-soluble, permanent color system for the interior and exterior of buildings, rooms, and furniture. The paint comes in plastic cans and drums in pint, quart, and gallon sizes. There are fifty glorious colors, all available in flat, semigloss, and patent-leather-gloss finishes.

The exhibit should demonstrate the practicability and beauty of this new product. This should be a modular type of exhibit, consisting of several panels made into exterior and interior shapes and forms. Panels can interlock and be arranged in different floor plans, depending on the size of the exhibit. A permanent display of colorful plastic cans (your design) of all sizes should be prominently placed with informative copy and color charts.

The final structure is made of lightweight interlocking panels. A styrene or Fome-Cor scale model should be developed and built on a scale of one-half inch to one foot.

This is a highly realistic project. It should demonstrate the power and impact of introducing and marketing color through an exhibit. The additional feature of the exhibit is the permanent display of products. The display will be distributed to major paint and hardware stores.

Books and Publications

Creative, The Magazine of Promotion and Marketing.

Hanlon, Al. **Trade Shows in the Marketing Mix.** Boston, Mass.: Herman Publishing, Inc., 1981.

Hayett, William. **Display and Exhibit Handbook.** N.Y., N.Y.: Reinhold Publishing Corp., 1967.

Industrial Design magazine.

Interiors magazine.

Manufacturers, Distributors, and Designers of Ready-Made Exhibits

Abstracta Structures, Inc.
38 West 39th Street
New York, N.Y. 10018

The Channel-kor System
P.O. Box 2297
Bloomington, Ind. 47402

Modtek Modular Units
Contempo Design, Inc.
3550 Woodhead Drive
Northbrook, Ill. 60062

Mod-U-Pac Display Specialties
6961 Hayvehurst Avenue
Van Nuys, Calif. 91406

Sell-Pac-80
The Derse Company
P.O. Box 959
Racine, Wisc. 53405

Unicube Corp.
540 Manida Street
Bronx, N.Y. 10474

Appendixes

Industry Organizations

NADI—National Association of Display Industries
120 East 23rd Street
New York, N.Y. 10010

POPAI—Point-of-Purchase Advertising Institute, Inc.
60 East 42nd Street
New York, N.Y. 10017

ASID—American Society of Interior Designers
730 Fifth Avenue
New York, N.Y. 10019

PDC—Package Designers Council (Package
and Industrial Designers)
P.O. Box 3753
New York, N.Y. 10017

AIA—American Institute of Architects
Your local chapter

Professional Publications

Visual Merchandising
407 Gilbert Avenue
Cincinnati, Ohio 45202

Creative, The magazine of promotion and marketing
37 West 39th Street
New York, N.Y. 10018

Industrial Design magazine
717 Fifth Avenue
New York, N.Y. 10022

Interiors
1515 Broadway
New York, N.Y. 10036

American Craft
401 Park Avenue South
New York, N.Y. 10016

Schools and Colleges

Most colleges offer a comprehensive design program for
beginner designers. The following colleges offer special
programs for designers interested in display and display-
related design, interior and environmental design, package
and point-of-purchase design, industrial and graphic
design.

Art Center College of Design
1700 Lida Street
Pasadena, Calif. 91103

California State University
800 N. State College Blvd.
Fullerton, Calif. 92634

University of California
405 Hilgard Avenue
Los Angeles, Calif. 90024

The Columbus College of Art and Design
47 N. Washington Avenue
Columbus, Ohio 43215

Massachussetts College of Art
364 Brookline Avenue
Boston, Mass. 02215

University of Michigan, School of Art
2000 Bonisteel Blvd.
Ann Arbor, Mich. 48109

Art Institute of Philadelphia
1622 Chestnut Street
Philadelphia, Pa. 19103

Philadelphia College of Art
Broad & Spruce Streets
Philadelphia, Pa. 19102

Rhode Island School of Design
2 College Street
Providence, R.I. 02903

Yale University, School of Art
180 York Street
New Haven, Conn. 06520

School of Visual Arts
209 East 23rd Street
New York, N.Y. 10010

Fashion Institute of Technology
227 West 27th Street
New York, N.Y. 10001

Pratt-Phoenix School of Design
160 Lexington Avenue
New York, N.Y. 10016

Parsons School of Design
66 Fifth Avenue
New York, N.Y. 10011

University of Wisconsin-Stout
Menomonie, Wisc. 54751

Rochester Institute of Technology
Rochester, N.Y. 14623

Syracuse University, Schools of Art,
Architecture, and Communications
Syracuse, N.Y. 13210

Services and Suppliers

Mannequins

D.G. Williams, Inc.
498 Seventh Avenue
New York, N.Y. 10018

Herzberg-Robbins, Inc.
209 West 38th Street
New York, N.Y. 10012

Adel Rootstein
451 West Broadway
New York, N.Y. 10012

F.W. Mannequin Arts
11946 Wagner Street
Culver City, Calif. 90230

Goldsmith Mannequins
10-09 43rd Avenue
Long Island City, N.Y. 11101

Greneker Mannequins
47 West 34th Street
New York, N.Y. 10001

Display Fixtures and Forms

LOR Sales Company
11 West 24th Street
New York, N.Y. 10011

Jerry Roe Enterprises
432 Austen Place
Bronx, N.Y. 10455

Henry Margau Wigs
540 Commerce Drive
Yeadon, Pa. 19050

Merchandise Presentation, Inc.
3960 Merritt Avenue
Bronx, N.Y. 10466

Roberts Colonial House
570 VM West 167 St.
South Holland, Ill. 60473

Edron Fixture Corp.
12 West 37th Street
New York, N.Y. 10018

Irving Fixture Corp.
25 Grant Avenue
Copague, N.Y. 11726

Human Form Hanger & Display
6101 16th Avenue
Brooklyn, N.Y. 11204

Jay Display & Fixture Corp.
1045 10th Avenue
San Diego, Calif. 92101

Lafayette Display Fixtures
100 Hinsdale Street
Brooklyn, N.Y. 11207

Magic Glass
668 Guerrero Street
San Francisco, Calif. 94110

Manhattan Store Interiors, Inc.
17 Moultrie Street
Brooklyn, N.Y. 11222

Leo Prager, Inc.
155 West 23rd Street
New York, N.Y. 10011

Royal Display Products Corp.
71 West 23rd Street
New York, N.Y. 10010

Sel-O-Rak Corporation
3580 Northwest 52nd Street
Miami, Fla. 33142

Target Supply and Display Inc.
321 Fifth Avenue
New York, N.Y. 10016

Unicube Corp.
540 Manida Street
Bronx, N.Y. 10474

Abstracta Structures
38 West 39th Street
New York, N.Y. 10018

Fabrics

Dazians, Inc.
40 East 29th Street
New York, N.Y. 10016

Circle Fabrics
16 West 36th Street
New York, N.Y. 10018

Trim Corporation of America
10 West 20th Street
New York, N.Y. 10011

Central Shippee, Inc. "The Felt People"
Bloomingdale, N.J. 07403

Fabulous Felt by Beckman
120 Baxter Street
New York, N.Y. 10013

Artificial Flowers, Decorations, and Displays

Lion Ribbon Company, Inc.
225 Fifth Avenue
New York, N.Y. 10010

James A. Cole, Inc.
675 Avenue of the Americas
New York, N.Y. 10010

Arty Flower Importers
2278 Monitor Street
Dallas, Texas 75207

Chic Displays
142 West 14th Street
New York, N.Y. 10011

Bliss Display Inc.
37-21 32nd Street
Long Island City, N.Y. 11101

Colonial Decorative Display Co. Inc.
122 West 26th Street
New York, N.Y. 10001

Holiday Decorations
3320 Lawson Blvd.
Oceanside, N.Y. 11572

Hub Floral Corp.
53 Fargo Street
Boston, Mass. 02210

David Hamberger, Inc.
136 West 31st Street
New York, N.Y. 10011

Austen Display Corp.
139 West 19th Street
New York, N.Y. 10011

National Decorators Supply Co. Inc.
443 Virginia Avenue
Indianapolis, Ind. 46203

Christmas Lights and Decorations

Kurt S. Adler, Inc.
1107 Broadway
New York, N.Y. 10010

American Christmas Decorating Inc.
30-28 Starr Avenue
Long Island City, N.Y. 11101

Arts and Flowers Displays
234 West 56th Street
New York, N.Y. 10022

Noma Worldwide, Inc.
200 Fifth Avenue
New York, N.Y. 10010

Animation

Garrison Wagner, Inc.
2018 Washington Street
St. Louis, Mo. 63103

All Season Display Company
24 Vampum
Park Ridge, N.J. 07656

Banners

National Banner Co. Inc.
11938 Harry Hines Blvd.
Dallas, Texas 75234

Ace Banner and Flag Co.
107 West 27th Street
New York, N.Y. 10001

Lighting

Electra, Inc.
122 West 27th Street
New York, N.Y. 10001

Lighting Services Inc.
150 East 58th Street
New York, N.Y. 10022

Times Square Theatrical Lighting Co. Inc.
318 West 47th Street
New York, N.Y. 10036

Festive Illuminations, Inc.
16 Engineers Road
Roslyn Harbor, N.Y. 11576

Sunormoon Industries, Inc.
831 West Davis
Dallas, Texas 75208

Signs and Letters

Mitten Designer Letters
85 Fifth Avenue
New York, N.Y. 10003, and
Redlands, Calif. 92373

Scott Plastic Co., Inc.
P.O. Box 2958
Sarasota, Florida 33578

Polyplastic Forms, Inc.
49 Gazza Blvd.
Farmingdale, N.Y. 11735

Simco Sign Studios
40 S Mac Dade Blvd.
Glenolden, Pa. 19036

Artkraft Strauss Sign Corporation
830 12th Avenue
New York, N.Y. 10019

Background Papers

Eastern Artist and Drafting Materials Inc.
352 Park Avenue South
New York, N.Y. 10010

The BD Company
2011 West 12th Street
Erie, Pa. 16512

Etcetera Wallpapers
22-78 35th Street
Long Island City, N.Y. 11105

MSC Paper Products
777 Ramsey Avenue
Hillside, N.J. 07205

Boards, Panels, and Plastics

Charette Corporation
212 East 54th Street
New York, N.Y. 10022

Garrison Wagner, Inc.
2018 Washington Street
St. Louis, Mo. 63103

Ain Plastics, Inc.
160 Mac Questen Parkway, P.O. Box 151
Mount Vernon, N.Y. 10550

Art Supplies

Sam Flax Inc.
25 East 28th Street
New York, N.Y. 10016

Arthur Brown & Bros. Inc.
2 West 46th Street
New York, N.Y. 10016

A.I. Friedman, Inc.
25 West 45th Street
New York, N.Y. 10036

You may ask for an illustrated catalog of art materials from these large art supply stores located in New York City. They accept mail orders. Catalogs must be requested on business or school stationery.

Glossary

accordion fold A zigzag arrangement of panels that can fold flat or be stretched wide, depending on space requirements.

acetate Flexible plastic film; it comes in clear and in colors in various thicknesses (gauges).

acrylic A plastic resin. Water-soluble paint, available in a wide range of colors. Also available as a plastic sheet and rod under the trade names of Lucite, Plexiglas.

angled front Store window that parallels the sidewalk but angles away from the sidewalk contour.

arcade front Store window open in sweep, often combined with island-type windows.

audiovisual The use of sound and image to convey or present a message, usually by projection of films or slides.

bevel A slanting edge on a frame or mat.

bin A display holder of bulk merchandise.

blacklight An ultraviolet type of fluorescent (or bulb) light that glows in the dark.

bleed A term describing art or copy that runs off the trimmed edge of the page (e.g., a poster without a margin is a bleed poster).

blister pack A card containing an item sealed under a plastic casing.

blowup A mechanical enlargement of art or copy.

bottle topper A small display card designed for the neck of a bottle; it carries a sales message.

boutique A specialty shop, selling fashions and accessories.

brayer A hard rubber hand roller used to rub down material mounted with adhesive. Brayers are also used to spread pigments for printing.

burlap Inexpensive, loosely woven fabric with coarse texture. Comes in many colors.

burnisher A tool to rub down pressure type.

Cello-Tak® Trade name for a transparent rub-on color overlay sheet. Available in 150 hues.

chip board Inexpensive, gray, uncoated board.

Color-Aid® Trade name for a line of silk-screened papers available in many matte colors.

comprehensive (or "comp") A semifinished piece of art or model.

copy A printed advertising message.

Corobuff® Trade name for a flexible corrugated paper.

corrugated Semirigid paperboard with fluted paper core. Flutes come in A, B, C, and E thicknesses. There is also a plastic corrugated board that comes in many colors, opaque and translucent.

counter card A small poster with easel, designed for counters.

counter display A small display especially designed for counters.

Cutawl® Trade name for a mechanical cutting device.

cut-case A shipping carton designed to be cut into shelf trays.

coupon pad A deck of serrated coupons attached to a display that features mail-in premiums.

crop To trim or cut off parts of art or photo.

crow's feet A metal bracket or wires that fit into a pole and form the feet of a pole display.

Day-Glo® A series of fluorescent paints, inks, and papers.

deal An offer by the advertiser, or an incentive for the merchant.

decal Short for decalcomania. A transfer printed on plastic or paper, to be transferred to objects.

die cutting Cutting out special shapes by means of a die.

diorama A miniature stage or a dimensional exhibit or display.

display carton Carton designed to fold out into a display.

double-back tape Tape with adhesive on both sides.

dowel A plastic or wood rod.

drop test Testing display, package, or product for shipping.

dry mounting Permanent mounting done with dry-mounting press or with special cement or waxes.

dry transfer Rub-down type or image.

dummy A) A shape like a person, B) a mock-up of a display or model, C) merchandise: empty boxes or bottles, containers for display.

duvetyne Inexpensive, soft display fabric for backgrounds and fixtures.

easel A vertical strut of cardboard that holds a card or display poster upright.

embossing A process of raising prints, designs, and patterns.

embossing plate A deep-etched metal plate to emboss with.

end-aisle display A display especially built to be placed at the end of the aisle to hold merchandise.

epoxy An exceedingly powerful plastic adhesive.

expanded polystyrene A lightweight foamlike plastic. Excellent material for insulating, packaging, and display work.

extrusion The method of making rods and tubes from plastics.

eyelet Metal or plastic reinforcing ring, through which wire or string can be drawn.

facile paper A paper covered with a satinlike fabric layer.

fixative A chemical spray that prevents smearing.

flasher A light that flashes on and off to attract attention.

Flicker flame® A trade name for an electric bulb that simulates flickering candle flame.

flint paper A glossy, smooth paper that comes in a wide range of beautiful colors. Also known as glazed paper.

flocking A spraying process to produce velvetlike texture.

foil Paper and cardboard with a thin layer of metal foil (available in many colors) laminated to the outer layer of the paper.

Fome-Cor® Trade name for a laminated lightweight board with a porous polystyrene foam core.

font An assortment of alphabet characters of one size and style.

four-color process Printing that reproduces a wide range of color by printing four colors in sequence, one over the other.

French curve A variety of curved templates in graceful patterns.

frisket A film mask used to cover areas of artwork that are not to be affected by a paint spray.

glitter Shiny decorative particles to be adhered to display materials. Often called diamond dust.

gondola Island shelving, open on two sides, common to self-service stores. Often supplied with gondola topper, a sign that can be seen on both sides.

grain The direction of fibers in a cardboard. The grain will affect the direction in which the board will sag or warp.

gravity-fed A display designed so that the force of gravity will bring more products into view.

grommet See **Eyelet**.

header A message board projecting above a display for the advertising message or headline.

heat motor A small rotating motion element that is operated by the heat of an electric bulb.

Homosote® A manufactured soft construction board. Useful for display panels and bulletin boards.

hot stamping A process by which a piece of artwork or copy is stamped onto any surface by heating a metal die which in turn heats a foil or color.

injection molding A process which consists of injecting plastics into a mold. Involves high preparatory mold costs. For large quantities only.

insert An advertisement packaged with retail merchandise.

instant lettering See: **Dry transfer.**

instruction sheet Printed, illustrated step-by-step instructions on how to set up or assemble a display.

island unit A display or exhibit designed to be viewed from all sides.

laminating The process used to adhere, mount, attach, or coat.

Latex® Trade name for a rubber molding material.

light box A) A display unit that houses a color transparency, B) an illuminated, frosted-glass-topped box used to trace artwork.

linkage A mechanical arrangement of moving parts in a motion display.

locks For display and packages. Tabs to lock into slots in order to secure or close sections.

logo The advertiser's stylized trade name or trademark.

Lucite® Trade name for an acrylic plastic.

Luxo® Trade name for a lamp that uses either incandescent bulbs or fluorescent tubes.

make ready The final preparation for production: printing, molding, die cutting, etc.

mannequin A lifelike figure used in stores to display clothing.

markers Plastic- or felt-tipped transparent dye applicators.

masking tape An opaque adhesive tape.

Masonite® Trade name for a hardboard panel.

master carton A shipping carton used to pack several cartons of merchandise.

mat A cardboard frame or window for photos or artwork. Mats are cut out of mat boards.

mat knife An adjustable knife with replaceable blade.

mechanical Artwork or type pasted into position for reproduction.

merchandiser A display containing merchandise for sale.

miniature A small-scale model.

mobile A display consisting of several counterbalanced pieces suspended in such a way that each piece moves independently in a light current of air.

mock-up A rough idea or sample of a construction or structural design.

modular A system permitting the building of displays or exhibits from a few basic units (modules).

mold Three-dimensional patterns or forms from which products can be molded from various materials.

monk's cloth A basket-weave fabric used for exhibit backgrounds.

montage An arrangement of graphic elements used to create a total visual effect.

mounting and finishing Joining parts of displays or assembly.

Mylar® Trade name for a bright metallic plastic film.

offset printing A method of printing in which impressions are transferred from the engraving plate to a rubber blanket and then printed on paper.

open-back windows Store windows open to the ground-floor area.

overrun Additional copies of printed material beyond the number ordered (usually 5%).

pantograph An instrument used to enlarge or reduce art.

pantone papers® A range of 563 colors and transparent color overlays most suitable for comprehensives and graphic design.

papier-mâché A sculpture medium consisting of paper and glue over an armature or cast from a mold.

paste-up See: **Mechanical.**

pegboard Perforated hardboard with rows of holes; can be used with a variety of metal fittings.

permanent display A display designed to remain for an indefinite length of time.

photostat A photocopy made with special photographic equipment.

Plexiglas® Trade name for a glasslike transparent acrylic plastic.

ply A thickness or layer.

pole topper A display that is mounted at the top of a pole.

POP Abbreviation for point-of-purchase advertising.

pop-up A display or mailing piece in which an element automatically pops up.

poster colors Often called show-card colors or tempera. Opaque, water-based colors.

prepack A display designed to be packed with merchandise by the advertiser and shipped as a unit.

pressure-sensitive Refers to papers, labels, and die-cut letters with special adhesive backing.

process color The four basic printing inks: yellow, magenta, blue, and black.

prototype Hand-made scale model, or a model for production.

public-service display Clocks, menus, and thermometers, for example, that serve and inform the public.

pump topper Display used on top of gasoline pumps.

rack A floor stand featuring shelves and pockets, to hold a variety of merchandise. They often revolve, and are mostly made of wire.

rear projection A method of projecting on the back of a screen. There are portable units made for sales presentation and for exhibits.

release A written permission to use a photo or artwork.

retouching To correct, change, or alter a photograph.

riser Often called a **reader**—a card or poster positioned on the top of a display.

rubber-plate printing Usually on corrugated board. An inexpensive method.

scale model A miniature representation where the size has been reduced proportionately.

score To press a blunt tool into board so that the board can be bent.

screw eye A screw with a loop or eye.

seamless paper Extra-wide, heavy paper with nonreflective surface. Used for photographic backgrounds. Comes in eight- and twelve-foot widths and in many colors.

serigraph See: **Silk-screen process.**

shadowbox A small, shallow showcase.

shelf extender A display in the form of a tray to attach to a shelf.

shelf talker A printed, often die-cut, card attached to the shelf.

silk-screen process A process of reproducing original art by using a fine mesh screen through which paint is pushed or squeegeed to make an impression.

slip sheet A paper or board separator between printed displays or posters.

Sobo® Trade name for an all-purpose adhesive, most suitable for fabrics, wood, and paper.

spray booth A small chamber with a reverse fan for safe and efficient spraying.

squeegee A hard rubber blade used to push paint through a silk screen.

stencil A piece of cardboard with a perforated letter or design. Stencils are also often made of thin metal or plastics.

stitch To fasten display parts with wire staples.

streamer An unmounted poster-type display used in supermarkets.

strip To remove die cuts from the board.

tag stock A thin, flexible cardboard.

template An outline of letters and shapes, usually made of transparent plastics.

tent A display card folded in half like an inverted **V**, with copy on both sides.

tester A small counter display bearing the actual product, which the consumer is encouraged to test.

tie-in Cooperative advertising effort where products are featured together in one display unit. Products are sometimes from different manufacturers.

tip-on Art or swatches glued or stapled to a card or display.

tooling Tooling up refers to the process of readying facilities for mass production (dies, molds, and equipment).

tracing paper A thin, semitransparent paper for tracing.

transparency A chrome; a transparent photograph in full color.

triptych A three-panel display or exhibit structure.

type C print A full-color photoprint used for exhibits.

vacuum forming Often called thermoforming. An inexpensive process by which plastic signs, blister packages, and displays are shaped with heat and vacuum.

visual merchandising Another name for retail displays.

X-Acto® Trade name for a line of cutting tools.

Index